ACCOUNTING WORKBOOK

for

QuickBooks®
2000

CHAPTERS 4-16

Prepared by

Warren Allen and *Mary Allen*

Problem Material Prepared by

James A. Heintz
University of Kansas

and

Robert W. Parry
Indiana University

SOUTH-WESTERN
THOMSON LEARNING™

Australia · Canada · Mexico · Singapore · Spain · United Kingdom · United States

Accounting Workbook for Quickbooks® 2000

Acquisitions Editor: Scott Person
Developmental Editors: Sara Wilson and Mardell Toomey
Marketing Manager: Larry Qualls
Production Editor: Marci Dechter
Editorial Assistant: Sara Froelicher
Manufacturing Coordinator: Doug Wilke
Production House: Navta Associates
Cover Design: Patti Hudepohl/Ft. Thomas, KY
Cover Image: PhotoDisc, Inc.
Printer: Globus

Printed in the United States of America
1 2 3 4 5 04 03 02 01

For more information contact South-Western, 5101 Madison Road, Cincinnati, Ohio, 45227 or find us on the Internet at http://www.swcollege.com
For permission to use material from this text or product, contact us by
- telephone: 1-800-730-2214
- fax: 1-800-730-2215
- web: http://www.thomsonrights.com

0-324-12396-5

CONTENTS

SECTION 3   SETTING UP A NEW COMPANY

SECTION 4   DEMONSTRATION PROBLEM SOLUTIONS

SECTION 1

Installing the Quickbooks Data Files

INSTALLING THE QUICKBOOKS DATA FILES

The opening balance files for selected problems are included on the QuickBooks Accounting CD. Each problem requires a unique data file containing the opening balance data for that problem. To solve a particular problem, you will restore the data file that contains the opening balances. As you solve the problem, the computer will be updating information in the restored file; therefore, each user must have his or her own unique copy of the respective file. The step-by-step instructions for installing the QuickBooks Data Files are detailed below:

▶ **Place the QuickBooks Accounting CD into the CD-ROM drive.**

▶ **Select Start, then Run. Type the command to run the setup program, casetup.exe from the CD-ROM drive (e.g., D:\QBSETUP, assuming the CD-ROM is drive D).**

▶ **When the Welcome screen appears, click the Next button.**

▶ **The Select Components Window shown in Figure 1.1 allows you to select which of the available problems you wish to install.**

With this option, you can choose which files are to be installed. You can install the files for several chapters, just one chapter, or all the chapters. This option is especially useful if either available storage space is limited or it isn't always possible to access the same folder from one session to the next because the folder you need is on a different computer from one session to the next. Notice that each Chapter has a check mark next to it. The check mark indicates that the problems for that chapter will be installed. If you do not want the files for that chapter installed, click on the check mark to toggle it off.

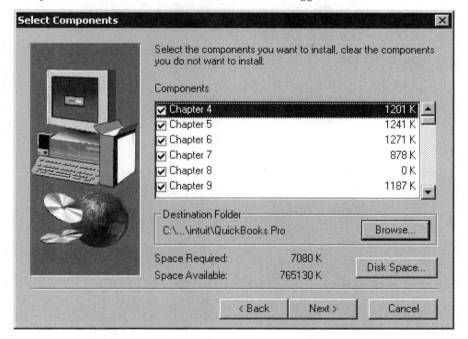

FIGURE 1.1 Select Components Window

▶ The default folder into which the data files will be installed is "Program Files\Intuit\QuickBooks Pro". This is the default folder for QuickBooks. To install into a different folder, click on the Browse button. When the Choose Folder window illustrated in Figure 1.2 appears, enter or select the drive and folder where you would like your file(s) to reside.

▶ Click on the Next button to proceed with the installation.

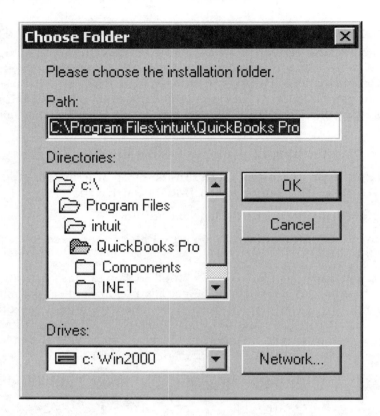

FIGURE 1.2 Choose Folder Window

When the Setup Complete dialog appears, click the Finish button.

SECTION 2

Instructions for Solving Selected Problems
Using QuickBooks Pro Software
Chapters 4-16

CHAPTER 4 DEMONSTRATION PROBLEM

George Fielding is a financial planning consultant. He provides budgeting, estate planning, tax planning, and investing advice for professional golfers. He developed the following chart of accounts for his business.

Assets
101 Cash
142 Office Supplies

Liabilities
202 Accounts Payable

Owner's Equity
311 George Fielding, Capital
312 George Fielding, Drawing

Revenues
401 Professional Fees

Expenses
511 Wages Expense
521 Rent Expense
525 Telephone Expense
533 Utilities Expense
534 Charitable Contributions Expense
538 Automobile Expense

The following transactions took place during the month of December of the current year.

Dec. 1   Fielding invested cash to start the business, $20,000.

3   Paid Bollhorst Real Estate for December office rent, $1,000.

4   Received cash from Aaron Patton, a client, for services, $2,500.

6   Paid T. Z. Anderson Electric for December heating and light, $75.

7   Received cash from Andrew Conder, a client, for services, $2,000.

12   Paid Fichter's Super Service for gasoline and oil purchases for the company car, $60.

14   Paid Hillenburg Staffing for temporary secretarial services during the past two weeks, $600.

17   Bought office supplies from Bowers Office Supply on account, $280.

20   Paid Mitchell Telephone Co. for business calls during the past month, $100.

21   Fielding withdrew cash for personal use, $1,100.

24   Made donation to the National Multiple Sclerosis Society, $100.

27   Received cash from Billy Walters, a client, for services, $2,000.

28   Paid Hillenburg Staffing for temporary secretarial services during the past two weeks, $600.

29   Made payment on account to Bowers Office Supply, $100.

Follow the step-by-step instructions below to complete the Chapter 4 Demonstration Problem.

STEP 1:   Start up the QuickBooks software.

Choose QuickBooks Pro from the Start button.

STEP 2: Restore the Opening Balance data for the Chapter 4 Demonstration Problem.

▶ From the File menu, choose Restore.

▶ When the Restore From window shown in Figure 2.1 appears, select "04 Demonstration Problem.QBB" and click on Open.

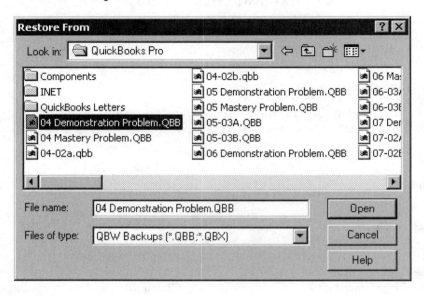

FIGURE 2.1 Restore From Window

▶ When the Restore To window shown in Figure 2.2 appears, use the Save in option to select the folder in which you wish to store your QuickBooks files, key a file name, and click on Save.

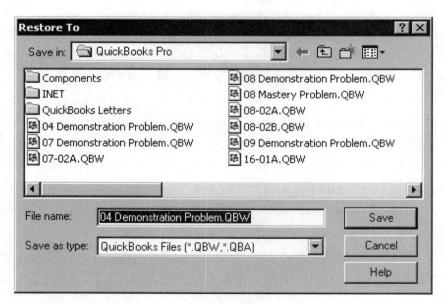

FIGURE 2.2 Restore To Window

The file name that you choose should identify the file as yours (04 Demo Jane Doe). QuickBooks will add an extension of QBW.

▶ If the file already exists, you will get a caution message. You must key "YES" and click OK to overwrite an existing file.

STEP 3: From the Company menu, choose the Make Journal Entry option and key the General Journal entries. You may leave the Entry No., Memo, and Name fields blank. Key the transactions for the month of December, 2002.

After each transaction has been keyed, click on Save & New to post and move to the next journal entry. To correct a previously entered journal entry, simply click on Previous until the entry you wish to correct appears, make corrections, and click on Save & New or Save & Close. The first journal entry is illustrated in the General Journal Entry window shown in Figure 2.3.

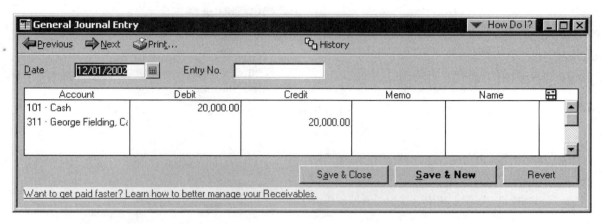

FIGURE 2.3 General Journal Entry Window

STEP 4: Display a General Journal report.

From the Reports menu, choose Memorized Reports. When the Memorized Reports list appears (see Figure 2.4), select General Journal Report and click on Generate Report.

FIGURE 2.4 Memorized Reports List Window

STEP 5: If errors are detected on the Journal report, return to the General Journal entries screen and make corrections.

STEP 6: Display the Trial Balance report.

From the Reports menu, choose Memorized Reports. Then, choose Trial Balance Report.

See the solution section of this workbook for the solution to this demonstration problem.

PROBLEM 4-2A

Annette Creighton opened Creighton Consulting. She rented a small office and paid a part-time worker to answer the telephone and make deliveries. Her chart of accounts is as follows:

Chart of Accounts

Assets
101 Cash
142 Office Supplies
181 Office Equipment

Liabilities
202 Accounts Payable

Owner's Equity
311 Annette Creighton, Capital
312 Annette Creighton, Drawing

Revenues
401 Consulting Fees

Expenses
511 Wages Expense
512 Advertising Expense
521 Rent Expense
525 Telephone Expense
526 Transportation Expense
533 Utilities Expense
549 Miscellaneous Expense

Creighton's transactions for the first month of business are as follows:

Jan. 1   Creighton invested cash in the business, $10,000.

1   Paid rent, $500.

2   Purchased office supplies on account, $300.

4   Purchased office equipment on account, $1,500.

6   Received cash for services rendered, $580.

7   Paid telephone bill, $42.

8   Paid utilities bill, $38.

10   Received cash for services rendered, $360.

12   Made payment on account, $50.

13   Paid for car rental while visiting an out-of-town client (transportation expense), $150.

15   Paid part-time worker, $360.

17   Received cash for services rendered, $420.

18   Creighton withdrew cash for personal use, $100.

20   Paid for a newspaper ad, $26.

22   Reimbursed part-time employee for cab fare incurred delivering materials to clients (transportation expense), $35.

24   Paid for books on consulting practices (miscellaneous expense), $28.

25   Received cash for services rendered, $320.

27   Made payment on account for office equipment purchased, $150.

29   Paid part-time worker, $360.

30   Received cash for services rendered, $180.

Follow the step-by-step instructions below to complete Problem 4-2A.

STEP 1:   Start up the QuickBooks software.

Choose QuickBooks Pro from the Start button.

STEP 2:   Restore the Opening Balance data for Problem 4-2A.

▶ From the File menu, choose Restore.

▶ When the Restore From window appears, select "04-02A.QBB" and click on Open.

▶ When the Restore To window appears, use the Save in option to select the folder in which you wish to store your QuickBooks files, key a file name, and click on Save.

   The file name that you choose should identify the file as yours (04-02A Jane Doe). QuickBooks will add an extension of QBW.

▶ If the file already exists, you will get a caution message. You must key "YES" and click OK to overwrite an existing file.

STEP 3:   From the Company menu, choose the Make Journal Entry option and key the General Journal entries. You may leave the Entry No., Memo, and Name fields blank. Key the transactions for the month of January, 2002.

   After each transaction has been keyed, click on Save & New to post and move to the next journal entry. To correct a previously entered journal entry, simply click on Previous until the entry you wish to correct appears, make corrections, and click on Save & New or Save & Close.

STEP 4:   Display a General Journal report.

   From the Reports menu, choose Memorized Reports. When the Memorized Reports list appears, select General Journal Report and click on Generate Report.

STEP 5:   If errors are detected on the Journal report, return to the General Journal entries screen and make corrections.

STEP 6:   Display the Trial Balance report.

   From the Reports menu, choose Memorized Reports. Then, choose Trial Balance Report.

PROBLEM 4-2B

Benito Mendez opened Mendez Appraisals. He rented office space and has a part-time secretary to answer the telephone and make appraisal appointments. His chart of accounts is as follows:

Chart of Accounts

Assets
101 Cash
122 Accounts Receivable
142 Office Supplies
181 Office Equipment

Liabilities
202 Accounts Payable

Owner's Equity
311 Benito Mendez, Capital
312 Benito Mendez, Drawing

Revenues
401 Appraisal Fees

Expenses
511 Wages Expense
512 Advertising Expense
521 Rent Expense
525 Telephone Expense
526 Transportation Expense
533 Electricity Expense
549 Miscellaneous Expense

Mendez's transactions for the first month of business are as follows:

May 1   Mendez invested cash in the business, $5,000.

    2   Paid rent, $500.

    3   Purchased office supplies, $100.

4	Purchased office equipment on account, $2,000.
5	Received cash for services rendered, $280.
8	Paid telephone bill, $38.
9	Paid electric bill, $42.
10	Received cash for services rendered, $310.
13	Paid part-time employee, $500.
14	Paid car rental for out-of-town trip, $200.
15	Paid for newspaper ad, $30.
18	Received cash for services rendered, $620.
19	Paid mileage reimbursement for part-time employee's use of personal car for business deliveries (transportation expense), $22.
21	Mendez withdrew cash for personal use, $50.
23	Made payment on account for office equipment purchased earlier, $200.
24	Earned appraisal fee, which will be paid in a week, $500.
26	Paid for newspaper ad, $30.
27	Paid for local softball team sponsorship (miscellaneous expense), $15.
28	Paid part-time employee, $500.
29	Received cash on account, $250.
30	Received cash for services rendered, $280.
31	Paid cab fare (transportation expense), $13.

Follow the step-by-step instructions below to complete the Problem 4-2B.

STEP 1:   Start up the QuickBooks software.

Choose QuickBooks Pro from the Start button.

STEP 2:   Restore the Opening Balance data for Problem 4-2B.

▶ **From the File menu, choose Restore.**

▶ **When the Restore From window appears, select "04-02B.QBB" and click on Open.**

▶ **When the Restore To window appears, use the Save in option to select the folder in which you wish to store your QuickBooks files, key a file name, and click on Save.**

The file name that you choose should identify the file as yours (04-02B Jane Doe). QuickBooks will add an extension of QBW.

▶ **If the file already exists, you will get a caution message. You must key "YES" and click OK to overwrite an existing file.**

STEP 3:   From the Company menu, choose the Make Journal Entry option and key the General Journal entries. You may leave the Entry No., Memo, and Name fields blank. Key the transactions for the month of May, 2002.

After each transaction has been keyed, click on Save & New to post and move to the next journal entry. To correct a previously entered journal entry, simply click on Previous until the entry you wish to correct appears, make corrections, and click on Save & New or Save & Close.

STEP 4:   Display a General Journal report.

From the Reports menu, choose Memorized Reports. When the Memorized Reports list appears, select General Journal Report and click on Generate Report.

STEP 5:   **If errors are detected on the Journal report, return to the General Journal entries screen and make corrections.**

STEP 6:   Display the Trial Balance report.

From the Reports menu, choose Memorized Reports. Then, choose Trial Balance Report.

CHAPTER 4 MASTERY PROBLEM

Barry Bird opened the Barry Bird Basketball Camp for children ages 10 through 18. Campers typically register for one week in June or July, arriving on Sunday and returning home the following Saturday. College players serve as cabin counselors and assist the local college and high school coaches who run the practice sessions. The registration fee includes a room, meals at a nearby restaurant, and basketball instruction. In the off-season, the facilities are used for weekend retreats and coaching clinics. Bird developed the following chart of accounts for his service business.

Chart of Accounts

Assets
101 Cash
142 Office Supplies
183 Athletic Equipment
184 Basketball Facilities

Liabilities
202 Accounts Payable

Owner's Equity
311 Barry Bird, Capital
312 Barry Bird, Drawing

Revenues
401 Registration Fees

Expenses
511 Wages Expense
512 Advertising Expense
524 Food Expense
525 Telephone Expense
533 Utilities Expense
536 Postage Expense

The following transactions took place during the month of June.

June 1   Bird invested cash in the business, $10,000.

1   Purchased basketballs and other athletic equipment, $3,000.

2   Paid Hite Advertising for fliers that had been mailed to prospective campers, $5,000.

2   Collected registration fees, $15,000.

2   Rogers Construction completed work on a new basketball court that cost $12,000. Arrangements were made to pay the bill in July.

5   Purchased office supplies on account from Gordon Office Supplies, $300.

6   Received bill from Magic's Restaurant for meals served to campers on account, $5,800.

7   Collected registration fees, $16,200.

10   Paid wages to camp counselors, $500.

14   Collected registration fees, $13,500.

14   Received bill from Magic's Restaurant for meals served to campers on account, $6,200.

17	Paid wages to camp counselors, $500.
18	Paid postage, $85.
21	Collected registration fees, $15,200.
22	Received bill from Magic's Restaurant for meals served to campers on account, $6,500.
24	Paid wages to camp counselors, $500.
28	Collected registration fees, $14,000.
30	Received bill from Magic's Restaurant for meals served to campers on account, $7,200.
30	Paid wages to camp counselors, $500.
30	Paid Magic's Restaurant on account, $25,700.
30	Paid utility bill, $500.
30	Paid telephone bill, $120.
30	Bird withdrew cash for personal use, $2,000.

Follow the step-by-step instructions below to complete the Chapter 4 Mastery Problem.

STEP 1:   Start up the QuickBooks software.

Choose QuickBooks Pro from the Start button.

STEP 2:   Restore the Opening Balance data for the Chapter 4 Mastery Problem.

▶ **From the File menu, choose Restore.**

▶ **When the Restore From window appears, select "04 Mastery Problem.QBB" and click on Open.**

▶ **When the Restore To window appears, use the Save in option to select the folder in which you wish to store your QuickBooks files, key a file name, and click on Save.**

The file name that you choose should identify the file as yours (04 Mastery Jane Doe). QuickBooks will add an extension of QBW.

▶ **If the file already exists, you will get a caution message. You must type "YES" and click OK to overwrite an existing file.**

STEP 3:   From the Company menu, choose the Make Journal Entry option and key the General Journal entries. You may leave the Entry No., Memo, and Name fields blank. Key the transactions for the month of June, 2002.

After each transaction has been keyed, click on Save & New to post and move to the next journal entry. To correct a previously entered journal entry, simply click on Previous until the entry you wish to correct appears, make corrections, and click on Save & New or Save & Close.

STEP 4:   Display a General Journal report.

From the Reports menu, choose Memorized Reports. When the Memorized Reports list appears, select General Journal Report and click on Generate Report.

STEP 5:   If errors are detected on the Journal report, return to the General Journal entries screen and make corrections.

STEP 6:   Display the Trial Balance report.

From the Reports menu, choose Memorized Reports. Then, choose Trial Balance Report.

CHAPTER 5 DEMONSTRATION PROBLEM

Justin Park is a lawyer specializing in corporate tax law. He began his practice on January 1. A chart of accounts and a trial balance taken on December 31, 2000 are shown below.

JUSTIN PARK LEGAL SERVICES
CHART OF ACCOUNTS

Assets		Revenue	
101	Cash	401	Client Fees
142	Office Supplies		
145	Prepaid Insurance	**Expenses**	
181	Office Equipment	511	Wages Expense
181.1	Accumulated Depr.—	521	Rent Expense
	Office Equipment	523	Office Supplies Expense
187	Computer Equipment	525	Telephone Expense
187.1	Accumulated Depr.—	533	Utilities Expense
	Computer Equipment	535	Insurance Expense
Liabilities		541	Depr. Expense—
201	Notes Payable		Office Equipment
202	Accounts Payable	542	Depr. Expense—
219	Wages Payable		Computer Equipment
Owner's Equity			
311	Justin Park, Capital		
312	Justin Park, Drawing		

Justin Park Legal Services
Trial Balance
December 31, 20 - -

ACCOUNT TITLE	ACCOUNT NO.	DEBIT BALANCE	CREDIT BALANCE
Cash	101	7 0 0 0 00	
Office Supplies	142	8 0 0 00	
Prepaid Insurance	145	1 2 0 0 00	
Office Equipment	181	15 0 0 0 00	
Computer Equipment	187	6 0 0 0 00	
Notes Payable	201		5 0 0 0 00
Accounts Payable	202		5 0 0 0 00
Justin Park, Capital	311		11 4 0 0 00
Justin Park, Drawing	312	5 0 0 0 00	
Client Fees	401		40 0 0 0 00
Wages Expense	511	12 0 0 0 00	
Rent Expense	521	5 0 0 0 00	
Telephone Expense	525	1 0 0 0 00	
Utilities Expense	533	3 9 0 0 00	
		56 9 0 0 00	56 9 0 0 00

Information for year-end adjustments is as follows:

(a) Office supplies on hand at year end amounted to $300.

(b) On January 1, 2000, Park purchased office equipment costing $15,000 with an expected life of five years and no salvage value.

(c) Computer equipment costing $6,000 with an expected life of three years and no salvage value was purchased on July 1, 2000. Assume that Park computes depreciation to the nearest full month.

(d) A premium of $1,200 for a one-year insurance policy was paid on December 1, 2000.

(e) Wages earned by Park's part-time secretary, which have not yet been paid, amount to $300.

Follow the step-by-step instructions below to complete the Chapter 5 Demonstration Problem.

STEP 1: **Start up the QuickBooks software.**

Choose QuickBooks Pro from the Start button.

STEP 2: **Restore the Opening Balance data for the Chapter 5 Demonstration Problem.**

▶ **From the File menu, choose Restore.**

▶ **When the Restore From window appears, select "05 Demonstration Problem.QBB" and click on Open.**

▶ **When the Restore To window appears, use the Save in option to select the folder in which you wish to store your QuickBooks files, key a file name, and click on Save.**

The file name that you choose should identify the file as yours (05 Demo Jane Doe). QuickBooks will add an extension of QBW.

▶ **If the file already exists, you will get a caution message. You must key "YES" and click OK to overwrite an existing file.**

STEP 3: **Display the Trial Balance report.**

From the Reports menu, choose Memorized Reports. Then, choose Trial Balance Report.

STEP 4: **Enter the adjusting entries for December 31, 2002 using the Make Journal Entry option. Key Adjusting Entry in the Memo field for each adjusting entry. The first adjusting entry is illustrated in the General Journal Entry window shown in Figure 2.5.**

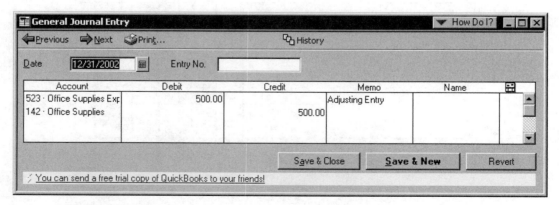

FIGURE 2.5 General Journal Entry Window

STEP 5: Display the adjusting entries using the General Journal Report option from the Memorized Reports list.

STEP 6: If errors are detected on the Journal report, return to the General Journal entries screen and make corrections.

STEP 7: Display the Income Statement Report from the Memorized Reports list.

STEP 8: Display the Balance Sheet Report from the Memorized Reports list.

See the solution section of this workbook for the solution to this demonstration problem.

PROBLEM 5-3A

Jason Armstrong started a business called Campus Escort Service. After the first month of operations, the trial balance as of November 30, 2000, is as shown below.
Information needed to make month-end adjustments follows:
(a) Ending inventory of supplies on November 30, $185.
(b) Unexpired (remaining) insurance as of November 30, $800.
(c) Depreciation expense on van, $300.
(d) Wages earned, but not paid as of November 30, $190.

Account Name	Account Number	Balance in Account Before Adjusting Entry
Supplies	141	$ 575
Prepaid Insurance	145	1,300
Accum. Depr.—Van	185.1	0
Wages Payable	219	0
Wages Expense	511	1,800
Supplies Expense	523	0
Insurance Expense	535	0
Depr. Expense—Van	541	0

Follow the step-by-step instructions below to complete Problem 5-3A.

STEP 1: Start up the QuickBooks software.

Choose QuickBooks Pro from the Start button.

STEP 2: Restore the Opening Balance data for Problem 5-3A.

▶ From the File menu, choose Restore.

▶ When the Restore From window appears, select "05-03A.QBB" and click on Open.

▶ When the Restore To window appears, use the Save in option to select the folder in which you wish to store your QuickBooks files, key a file name, and click on Save.

The file name that you choose should identify the file as yours (05-03A Jane Doe). QuickBooks will add an extension of QBW.

▶ If the file already exists, you will get a caution message. You must key "YES" and click OK to overwrite an existing file.

STEP 3: Display a Trial Balance report.

From the Reports menu, choose Memorized Reports. Then, choose Trial Balance Report.

STEP 4:   Enter the adjusting entries for November 30, 2002 using the Make Journal Entry option. Key Adjusting Entry in the Memo field for each adjusting entry.

STEP 5:   Display the adjusting entries using the General Journal Report option from the Memorized Reports list.

STEP 6:   If errors are detected on the Journal report, return to the General Journal entries screen and make corrections.

STEP 7:   Display the Income Statement Report from the Memorized Reports list.

STEP 8:   Display the Balance Sheet Report from the Memorized Reports list.

PROBLEM 5-3B

Val Nolan started a business called Nolan's Home Appraisals. The trial balance as of October 31, after the first month of operations, is shown below.

Information needed to make month-end adjustments follows:
  (a) Supplies inventory as of October 31, $210.
  (b) Unexpired (remaining) insurance as of October 31, $800.
  (c) Depreciation of automobile, $250.
  (d) Wages earned, but not paid as of October 31, $175.

Account Name	Account Number	Balance in Account Before Adjusting Entry
Supplies	141	$ 625
Prepaid Insurance	145	950
Accum. Depr.—Automobile	185.1	0
Wages Payable	219	0
Wages Expense	511	1,560
Supplies Expense	523	0
Insurance Expense	535	0
Depr. Expense—Automobile	541	0

Follow the step-by-step instructions below to complete Problem 5-3B.

STEP 1:   **Start up the QuickBooks software.**

Choose QuickBooks Pro from the Start button.

STEP 2:   **Restore the Opening Balance data for Problem 5-3B.**

▶ **From the File menu, choose Restore.**

▶ **When the Restore From window appears, select "05-03B.QBB" and click on Open.**

▶ **When the Restore To window appears, use the Save in option to select the folder in which you wish to store your QuickBooks files, key a file name, and click on Save.**

The file name that you choose should identify the file as yours (05-03B Jane Doe). QuickBooks will add an extension of QBW.

▶ **If the file already exists, you will get a caution message. You must key "YES" and click OK to overwrite an existing file.**

STEP 3: Display the Trial Balance report.

From the Reports menu, choose Memorized Reports. Then, choose Trial Balance Report.

STEP 4: Enter the adjusting entries for October 31, 2002 using the Make Journal Entry option. Key Adjusting Entry in the Memo field for each adjusting entry.

STEP 5: Display the adjusting entries using the General Journal Report option from Memorized Reports list.

STEP 6: If errors are detected on the Journal report, return to the General Journal entries screen and make corrections.

STEP 7: Display the Income Statement Report from the Memorized Reports list.

STEP 8: Display the Balance Sheet Report from the Memorized Reports list.

CHAPTER 5 MASTERY PROBLEM

Kristi Williams offers family counseling services specializing in financial and marital problems. A chart of accounts and a trial balance taken on December 31, 2000, on the next page.

Information for year-end adjustments:

(a) Office supplies on hand at year end amounted to $100.

(b) On January 1, 2000, Williams purchased office equipment that cost $18,000. It has an expected useful life of ten years and no salvage value.

(c) On July 1, 2000, Williams purchased computer equipment costing $6,000. It has an expected useful life of three years and no salvage value. Assume that Williams computes depreciation to the nearest full month.

(d) On December 1, 2000, Williams paid a premium of $600 for a six-month insurance policy.

Follow the step-by-step instructions below to complete the Chapter 5 Mastery Problem.

STEP 1: Start up the QuickBooks software.

Choose QuickBooks Pro from the Start button.

STEP 2: Restore the Opening Balance data for the Chapter 5 Mastery Problem.

▶ From the File menu, choose Restore.

▶ When the Restore From window appears, select "05 Mastery Problem.QBB" and click on Open.

▶ When the Restore To window appears, use the Save in option to select the folder in which you wish to store your QuickBooks files, key a file name, and click on Save.

The file name that you choose should identify the file as yours (05 Mastery Jane Doe). QuickBooks will add an extension of QBW.

▶ If the file already exists, you will get a caution message. You must key "YES" and click OK to overwrite an existing file.

STEP 3: Display the Trial Balance report.

From the Reports menu, choose Memorized Reports. Then, choose Trial Balance Report.

STEP 4: Enter the adjusting entries for December 31, 2002 using the Make Journal Entry option. Key Adjusting Entry in the Memo field for each adjusting entry.

KRISTI WILLIAMS FAMILY COUNSELING SERVICES
CHART OF ACCOUNTS

Assets		Revenue	
101	Cash	401	Client Fees
142	Office Supplies		
145	Prepaid Insurance	**Expenses**	
181	Office Equipment	511	Wages Expense
181.1	Accumulated Depr.—	521	Rent Expense
	Office Equipment	523	Office Supplies Expense
187	Computer Equipment	533	Utilities Expense
187.1	Accumulated Depr.—	535	Insurance Expense
	Computer Equipment	541	Depr. Expense—
			Office Equipment
Liabilities		542	Depr. Expense—
201	Notes Payable		Computer Equipment
202	Accounts Payable	549	Miscellaneous Expense
Owner's Equity			
311	Kristi Williams, Capital		
312	Kristi Williams, Drawing		

Kristi Williams Family Counseling Services
Trial Balance
December 31, 20 - 1

ACCOUNT TITLE	ACCOUNT NO.	DEBIT BALANCE					CREDIT BALANCE				
Cash	101	8	7	3	0	00					
Office Supplies	142		7	0	0	00					
Prepaid Insurance	145		6	0	0	00					
Office Equipment	181	18	0	0	0	00					
Computer Equipment	187	6	0	0	0	00					
Notes Payable	201						8	0	0	0	00
Accounts Payable	202							5	0	0	00
Kristi Williams, Capital	311						11	4	0	0	00
Kristi Williams, Drawing	312	3	0	0	0	00					
Client Fees	401						35	8	0	0	00
Wages Expense	511	9	5	0	0	00					
Rent Expense	521	6	0	0	0	00					
Utilities Expense	533	2	1	7	0	00					
Miscellaneous Expense	549	1	0	0	0	00					
		55	7	0	0	00	55	7	0	0	00

STEP 5: Display the adjusting entries using the General Journal option from the Memorized Reports list.

STEP 6: If errors are detected on the Journal report, return to the General Journal entries screen and make corrections.

STEP 7: Display the Income Statement Report from the Memorized Reports list.

STEP 8: Display the Balance Sheet Report from the Memorized Reports list.

CHAPTER 6 DEMONSTRATION PROBLEM

Follow the step-by-step instructions below to complete the Chapter 6 Demonstration Problem. Refer to the worksheet on the following page. Chang made no additional investments during the year.

STEP 1: Start up the QuickBooks software.

Choose QuickBooks Pro from the Start button.

STEP 2: Restore the Opening Balance data for the Chapter 6 Demonstration Problem.

▶ From the File menu, choose Restore.

▶ When the Restore From window appears, select "06 Demonstration Problem.QBB" and click on Open.

▶ When the Restore To window appears, use the Save in option to select the folder in which you wish to store your QuickBooks files, key a file name, and click on Save.

The file name that you choose should identify the file as yours (06 Demo Jane Doe). QuickBooks will add an extension of QBW.

▶ If the file already exists, you will get a caution message. You must key "YES" and click OK to overwrite an existing file.

STEP 3: Display the Trial Balance Report from the Memorized Reports list.

STEP 4: Enter the adjusting entries for December 31, 2002 using the Make Journal Entry option. Key Adjusting Entry in the Memo field for each adjusting entry. The first adjusting entry is illustrated in the General Journal Entry window shown in Figure 2.6.

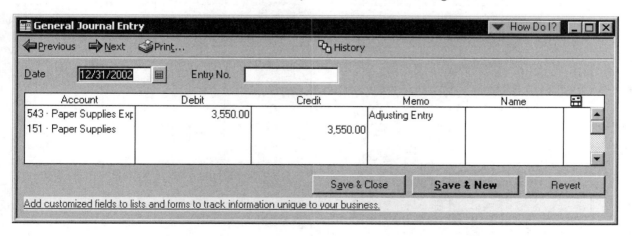

FIGURE 2.6 General Journal Entry Window

Hard Copy Printers
Work Sheet
For Year Ended December 31, 20- -

#	Account Title	Trial Balance Debit	Trial Balance Credit	Adjustments Debit	Adjustments Credit	Adjusted Trial Balance Debit	Adjusted Trial Balance Credit	Income Statement Debit	Income Statement Credit	Balance Sheet Debit	Balance Sheet Credit
1	Cash	11 8 0 0 00				11 8 0 0 00				11 8 0 0 00	
2	Paper Supplies	3 6 0 0 00			(a) 3 5 5 0 00	5 0 00				5 0 00	
3	Prepaid Insurance	1 0 0 0 00			(b) 5 0 5 00	4 9 5 00				4 9 5 00	
4	Printing Equipment	5 8 0 0 00				5 8 0 0 00				5 8 0 0 00	
5	Accum. Depr.—Printing Equipment				(d) 1 2 0 0 00		1 2 0 0 00				1 2 0 0 00
6	Accounts Payable		5 0 0 00				5 0 0 00				5 0 0 00
7	Wages Payable				(c) 3 0 00		3 0 00				3 0 00
8	Timothy Chang, Capital		10 0 0 0 00				10 0 0 0 00				10 0 0 0 00
9	Timothy Chang, Drawing	13 0 0 0 00				13 0 0 0 00				13 0 0 0 00	
10	Printing Fees		35 1 0 0 00				35 1 0 0 00		35 1 0 0 00		
11	Wages Expense	11 9 7 0 00		(c) 3 0 00		12 0 0 0 00		12 0 0 0 00			
12	Rent Expense	7 5 0 0 00				7 5 0 0 00		7 5 0 0 00			
13	Paper Supplies Expense			(a) 3 5 5 0 00		3 5 5 0 00		3 5 5 0 00			
14	Telephone Expense	5 5 0 00				5 5 0 00		5 5 0 00			
15	Utilities Expense	1 0 0 0 00				1 0 0 0 00		1 0 0 0 00			
16	Insurance Expense			(b) 5 0 5 00		5 0 5 00		5 0 5 00			
17	Depr. Expense—Printing Equipment			(d) 1 2 0 0 00		1 2 0 0 00		1 2 0 0 00			
18		45 6 0 0 00	45 6 0 0 00	5 2 8 5 00	5 2 8 5 00	46 8 3 0 00	46 8 3 0 00	26 3 0 5 00	35 1 0 0 00	20 5 2 5 00	11 7 3 0 00
19	Net Income							8 7 9 5 00			8 7 9 5 00
20								35 1 0 0 00	35 1 0 0 00	20 5 2 5 00	20 5 2 5 00
21											
22											
23											
24											
25											
26											
27											
28											
29											
30											

STEP 5: Display the adjusting entries using the General Journal Report option from the Memorized Reports list.

STEP 6: If errors are detected on the Journal report, return to the General Journal entries screen and make corrections.

STEP 7: Display the Income Statement Report from the Memorized Reports list.

STEP 8: Display the Balance Sheet Report from the Memorized Reports list.

STEP 9: Display the Trial Balance Report from the Memorized Reports list.

STEP 10: Enter the closing entry to close the drawing account to capital on January 1, 2003. The closing entry is illustrated in the General Journal Entry window shown in Figure 2.7.

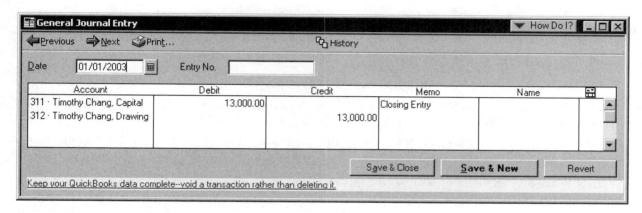

FIGURE 2.7 General Journal Entry Window

STEP 11: Display the Post-Closing Trial Balance Report from the Memorized Reports list.

It isn't necessary to make closing entries to close out revenue and expense accounts. QuickBooks controls the process by date. Notice that the trial balance report as of January 1, 2003 (the beginning of a new fiscal period) has the revenue and expense accounts closed to Capital.

See the Solution section of this workbook for the solution to this demonstration problem.

PROBLEM 6-3A

A chart of accounts for Monte's Repairs is provided below.

Monte's Repairs
Chart of Accounts

Assets
101   Cash
122   Accounts Receivable
141   Supplies
145   Prepaid Insurance
185   Delivery Equipment
185.1 Accum. Depr.—Delivery Equip.

Revenues
401   Repair Fees

Expenses
511   Wages Expense
512   Advertising Expense
521   Rent Expense
523   Supplies Expense

Liabilities
202 Accounts Payable
219 Wages Payable

Owner's Equity
311 Monte Eli, Capital
312 Monte Eli, Drawing
313 Income Summary

525 Telephone Expense
535 Insurance Expense
538 Gas and Oil Expense
541 Depr. Exp.—Delivery Equip.
549 Miscellaneous Expense

The processing for Problem 6-3A is somewhat different from the Chapter 6 Demonstration Problem because of a difference in the accounting period. The Demonstration Problem had a fiscal period of one year, whereas this problem has a fiscal period of one month. Follow the step-by-step procedures below to complete the processing for Problem 6-3A.

STEP 1: **Start up the QuickBooks software.**

Choose QuickBooks Pro from the Start button.

STEP 2: **Restore the Opening Balance data for Problem 6-3A.**

▶ **From the File menu, choose Restore.**

▶ **When the Restore From window appears, select "06-03A.QBB" and click on Open.**

▶ **When the Restore To window appears, use the Save in option to select the folder in which you wish to store your QuickBooks files, key a file name, and click on Save.**

The file name that you choose should identify the file as yours (06-03A Jane Doe). QuickBooks will add an extension of QBW.

▶ **If the file already exists, you will get a caution message. You must key "YES" and click OK to overwrite an existing file.**

STEP 3: **Display the Trial Balance Report from the Memorized Reports list.**

STEP 4: **Refer to the work sheet on the next page for adjusting entry information. Enter the adjusting entries for January 31, 2002 using the Make Journal Entry option. Key Adjusting Entry in the Memo field for each adjusting entry.**

STEP 5: **Display the adjusting entries using the General Journal Report option from the Memorized Reports list.**

STEP 6: **If errors are detected on the Journal report, return to the General Journal entries screen and make corrections.**

STEP 7: **Display the Income Statement Report from the Memorized Reports list.**

STEP 8: **Display the Balance Sheet Report from the Memorized Reports list.**

STEP 9: **Display the Trial Balance Report from the Memorized Reports list.**

STEP 10: **Enter the closing entry to close the drawing account to capital on February 1, 2002.**

STEP 11: **Display the Post-Closing Trial Balance Report from the Memorized Reports list.**

It isn't necessary to make closing entries to close out revenue and expense accounts. QuickBooks controls the process by date. Notice that the trial balance report as of February 1, 2002 (the beginning of a new fiscal period) has the revenue and expense accounts closed to Capital.

Monte's Repairs
Work Sheet
For Month Ended January 31, 20 --

	ACCOUNT TITLE	TRIAL BALANCE DEBIT	TRIAL BALANCE CREDIT	ADJUSTMENTS DEBIT	ADJUSTMENTS CREDIT	ADJUSTED TRIAL BALANCE DEBIT	ADJUSTED TRIAL BALANCE CREDIT	INCOME STATEMENT DEBIT	INCOME STATEMENT CREDIT	BALANCE SHEET DEBIT	BALANCE SHEET CREDIT
1	Cash	3 0 8 0 00				3 0 8 0 00				3 0 8 0 00	
2	Accounts Receivable	1 2 0 0 00				1 2 0 0 00				1 2 0 0 00	
3	Supplies	8 0 0 00			(a) 2 0 0 00	6 0 0 00				6 0 0 00	
4	Prepaid Insurance	9 0 0 00			(b) 1 0 0 00	8 0 0 00				8 0 0 00	
5	Delivery Equipment	3 0 0 0 00				3 0 0 0 00				3 0 0 0 00	
6	Accum. Depr.—Delivery Equipment				(d) 3 0 00		3 0 00				3 0 00
7	Accounts Payable		1 1 0 0 00				1 1 0 0 00				1 1 0 0 00
8	Wages Payable				(c) 1 5 0 00		1 5 0 00				1 5 0 00
9	Monte Eli, Capital		7 0 0 0 00				7 0 0 0 00				7 0 0 0 00
10	Monte Eli, Drawing	1 0 0 0 00				1 0 0 0 00				1 0 0 0 00	
11	Repair Fees		4 2 3 0 00				4 2 3 0 00		4 2 3 0 00		
12	Wages Expense	1 6 5 0 00		(c) 1 5 0 00		1 8 0 0 00		1 8 0 0 00			
13	Advertising Expense	1 7 0 00				1 7 0 00		1 7 0 00			
14	Rent Expense	4 2 0 00				4 2 0 00		4 2 0 00			
15	Supplies Expense			(a) 2 0 0 00		2 0 0 00		2 0 0 00			
16	Telephone Expense	4 9 00				4 9 00		4 9 00			
17	Insurance Expense			(b) 1 0 0 00		1 0 0 00		1 0 0 00			
18	Gas and Oil Expense	3 3 00				3 3 00		3 3 00			
19	Depr. Expense—Delivery Equipment			(d) 3 0 00		3 0 00		3 0 00			
20	Miscellaneous Expense	2 8 00				2 8 00		2 8 00			
21		12 3 3 0 00	12 3 3 0 00	4 8 0 00	4 8 0 00	12 5 1 0 00	12 5 1 0 00	2 8 3 0 00	4 2 3 0 00	9 6 8 0 00	8 2 8 0 00
22	Net Income							1 4 0 0 00			1 4 0 0 00
23								4 2 3 0 00	4 2 3 0 00	9 6 8 0 00	9 6 8 0 00
24											
25											
26											
27											
28											
29											
30											

PROBLEM 6-3B

A chart of accounts for Juanita's Consulting is provided below.

Juanita's Consulting
Chart of Accounts

Assets
101 Cash
122 Accounts Receivable
141 Supplies
145 Prepaid Insurance
181 Office Equipment
181.1 Accum. Depr.—Office Equip.

Liabilities
202 Accounts Payable
219 Wages Payable

Owner's Equity
311 Juanita Alvarez, Capital
312 Juanita Alvarez, Drawing
313 Income Summary

Revenues
401 Consulting Fees

Expense
511 Wages Expense
512 Advertising Expense
521 Rent Expense
523 Supplies Expense
525 Telephone Expense
533 Electricity Expense
535 Insurance Expense
538 Gas and Oil Expense
541 Depr. Exp.—Office Equip.
549 Miscellaneous Expense

Follow the step-by-step procedures below to complete the processing for Problem 6-3B.

STEP 1: Start up the QuickBooks software.

Choose QuickBooks Pro from the Start button.

STEP 2: Restore the Opening Balance data for Problem 6-3B.

▶ **From the File menu, choose Restore.**

▶ **When the Restore From window appears, select "06-03B.QBB" and click on Open.**

▶ **When the Restore To window appears, use the Save in option to select the folder in which you wish to store your QuickBooks files, key a file name, and click on Save.**

The file name that you choose should identify the file as yours (06-03B Jane Doe). QuickBooks will add an extension of QBW.

▶ **If the file already exists, you will get a caution message. You must key "YES" and click OK to overwrite an existing file.**

STEP 3: Display the Trial Balance Report from the Memorized Reports list.

STEP 4: Refer to the work sheet on the next page for adjusting entry information. Enter the adjusting entries for June 30, 2002 using the Make Journal Entry option. Key Adjusting Entry in the Memo field for each adjusting entry.

STEP 5: Display the adjusting entries using the General Journal Report option from the Memorized Reports list.

STEP 6: If errors are detected on the Journal report, return to the General Journal entries screen and make corrections.

STEP 7: Display the Income Statement Report from the Memorized Reports list.

STEP 8: Display the Balance Sheet Report from the Memorized Reports list.

Juanita's Consulting
Work Sheet
For Month Ended June 30, 20 - -

	ACCOUNT TITLE	TRIAL BALANCE DEBIT	TRIAL BALANCE CREDIT	ADJUSTMENTS DEBIT	ADJUSTMENTS CREDIT	ADJUSTED TRIAL BALANCE DEBIT	ADJUSTED TRIAL BALANCE CREDIT	INCOME STATEMENT DEBIT	INCOME STATEMENT CREDIT	BALANCE SHEET DEBIT	BALANCE SHEET CREDIT	
1	Cash	5 2 8 5 00				5 2 8 5 00				5 2 8 5 00		1
2	Accounts Receivable	1 0 7 5 00				1 0 7 5 00				1 0 7 5 00		2
3	Supplies	7 5 0 00			(a) 2 5 0 00	5 0 0 00				5 0 0 00		3
4	Prepaid Insurance	5 0 0 00			(b) 1 0 0 00	4 0 0 00				4 0 0 00		4
5	Office Equipment	2 2 0 0 00				2 2 0 0 00				2 2 0 0 00		5
6	Accum. Depr.—Office Equipment				(d) 1 1 0 00		1 1 0 00				1 1 0 00	6
7	Accounts Payable		1 5 0 0 00				1 5 0 0 00				1 5 0 0 00	7
8	Wages Payable				(c) 2 0 0 00		2 0 0 00				2 0 0 00	8
9	Juanita Alvarez, Capital		7 0 0 0 00				7 0 0 0 00				7 0 0 0 00	9
10	Juanita Alvarez, Drawing	8 0 0 00				8 0 0 00				8 0 0 00		10
11	Consulting Fees		4 2 0 4 00				4 2 0 4 00		4 2 0 4 00			11
12	Wages Expense	1 4 0 0 00		(c) 2 0 0 00		1 6 0 0 00		1 6 0 0 00				12
13	Advertising Expense	6 0 00				6 0 00		6 0 00				13
14	Rent Expense	5 0 0 00				5 0 0 00		5 0 0 00				14
15	Supplies Expense			(a) 2 5 0 00		2 5 0 00		2 5 0 00				15
16	Telephone Expense	4 6 00				4 6 00		4 6 00				16
17	Electricity Expense	3 9 00				3 9 00		3 9 00				17
18	Insurance Expense			(b) 1 0 0 00		1 0 0 00		1 0 0 00				18
19	Gas and Oil Expense	2 8 00				2 8 00		2 8 00				19
20	Depr. Expense—Office Equipment			(d) 1 1 0 00		1 1 0 00		1 1 0 00				20
21	Miscellaneous Expense	2 1 00				2 1 00		2 1 00				21
22		12 7 0 4 00	12 7 0 4 00	6 6 0 00	6 6 0 00	13 0 1 4 00	13 0 1 4 00	2 7 5 4 00	4 2 0 4 00	10 2 6 0 00	8 8 1 0 00	22
23	Net Income							1 4 5 0 00			1 4 5 0 00	23
24								4 2 0 4 00	4 2 0 4 00	10 2 6 0 00	10 2 6 0 00	24
25												25
26												26
27												27
28												28
29												29
30												30

STEP 9:   Display the Trial Balance Report from the Memorized Reports list.

STEP 10: Enter the closing entry to close the drawing account to capital on July 1, 2002.

STEP 11: Display the Post-Closing Trial Balance Report from the Memorized Reports list.

It isn't necessary to make closing entries to close out revenue and expense accounts. QuickBooks controls the process by date. Notice that the trial balance report as of July 1, 2002 (the beginning of a new fiscal period) has the revenue and expense accounts closed to Capital.

CHAPTER 6 MASTERY PROBLEM

In the Chapter 6 Mastery Problem, you will display the financial statements and close out the accounting period for Aunt Ibby's Styling Salon owned by Elizabeth Soltis. Follow the step-by-step instructions below to complete the Chapter 6 Mastery Problem. For Step 5, refer to the adjusting entry information in the work sheet on the next page.

STEP 1:   **Start up the QuickBooks software.**

Choose QuickBooks Pro from the Start button.

STEP 2:   **Restore the Opening Balance data for the Chapter 6 Mastery Problem.**

▶ **From the File menu, choose Restore.**

▶ **When the Restore From window appears, select "06 Mastery Problem.QBB" and click on Open.**

▶ **When the Restore To window appears, use the Save in option to select the folder in which you wish to store your QuickBooks files, key a file name, and click on Save.**

The file name that you choose should identify the file as yours (06 Mastery Jane Doe). QuickBooks will add an extension of QBW.

▶ **If the file already exists, you will get a caution message. You must key "YES" and click OK to overwrite an existing file.**

STEP 3:   **Display the Trial Balance Report.**

STEP 4:   **Enter the adjusting entries for December 31, 2002 using the Make Journal Entry option. Key Adjusting Entry in the Memo field for each adjusting entry.**

STEP 5:   **Display the adjusting entries using the General Journal Report option from the Memorized Reports list.**

STEP 6:   **If errors are detected on the Journal report, return to the General Journal entries screen and make corrections.**

STEP 7:   **Display the Income Statement Report from the Memorized Reports list.**

STEP 8:   **Display the Balance Sheet Report from the Memorized Reports list.**

STEP 9:   **Display the Trial Balance Report from the Memorized Reports list.**

STEP 10: **Enter the closing entry to close the drawing account to capital on January 1, 2003.**

STEP 11: **Display the Post-Closing Trial Balance Report from the Memorized Reports list.**

It isn't necessary to make closing entries to close out revenue and expense accounts. QuickBooks controls the process by date. Notice that the trial balance report as of January 1, 2003 (the beginning of a new fiscal period) has the revenue and expense accounts closed to Capital.

Aunt Ibby's Styling Salon
Work Sheet
For Year Ended December 31, 20--

	ACCOUNT TITLE	TRIAL BALANCE DEBIT	TRIAL BALANCE CREDIT	ADJUSTMENTS DEBIT	ADJUSTMENTS CREDIT	ADJUSTED TRIAL BALANCE DEBIT	ADJUSTED TRIAL BALANCE CREDIT	INCOME STATEMENT DEBIT	INCOME STATEMENT CREDIT	BALANCE SHEET DEBIT	BALANCE SHEET CREDIT	
1	Cash	9 4 0 0 00				9 4 0 0 00				9 4 0 0 00		1
2	Styling Supplies	1 5 0 0 00			(a) 1 4 5 0 00	5 0 00				5 0 00		2
3	Prepaid Insurance	8 0 0 00			(b) 6 5 0 00	1 5 0 00				1 5 0 00		3
4	Salon Equipment	4 5 0 0 00				4 5 0 0 00				4 5 0 0 00		4
5	Accum. Depr.—Salon Equipment				(d) 9 0 0 00		9 0 0 00				9 0 0 00	5
6	Accounts Payable		2 2 5 00				2 2 5 00				2 2 5 00	6
7	Wages Payable				(c) 4 0 00		4 0 00				4 0 00	7
8	Elizabeth Soltis, Capital		2 7 6 5 00				2 7 6 5 00				2 7 6 5 00	8
9	Elizabeth Soltis, Drawing	12 0 0 0 00				12 0 0 0 00				12 0 0 0 00		9
10	Styling Fees		32 0 0 0 00				32 0 0 0 00		32 0 0 0 00			10
11	Wages Expense	8 0 0 0 00		(c) 4 0 00		8 0 4 0 00		8 0 4 0 00				11
12	Rent Expense	6 0 0 0 00				6 0 0 0 00		6 0 0 0 00				12
13	Styling Supplies Expense			(a) 1 4 5 0 00		1 4 5 0 00		1 4 5 0 00				13
14	Telephone Expense	4 5 0 00				4 5 0 00		4 5 0 00				14
15	Utilities Expense	8 0 0 00				8 0 0 00		8 0 0 00				15
16	Insurance Expense			(b) 6 5 0 00		6 5 0 00		6 5 0 00				16
17	Depr. Expense—Salon Equipment			(d) 9 0 0 00		9 0 0 00		9 0 0 00				17
18		34 9 9 0 00	34 9 9 0 00	3 0 4 0 00	3 0 4 0 00	35 9 3 0 00	35 9 3 0 00	18 2 9 0 00	32 0 0 0 00	17 6 4 0 00	3 9 3 0 00	18
19	Net Income							13 7 1 0 00			13 7 1 0 00	19
20								32 0 0 0 00	32 0 0 0 00	17 6 4 0 00	17 6 4 0 00	20
21												21
22												22
23												23
24												24
25												25
26												26
27												27
28												28
29												29
30												30

COMPREHENSIVE PROBLEM 1

Bob Night opened The General's Favorite Fishing Hole. The fishing camp is open from April through September and attracts many famous college basketball coaches during the off-season. Guests typically register for one week, arriving on Sunday afternoon and returning home the following Saturday afternoon. The registration fee includes room and board, the use of fishing boats, and professional instruction in fishing techniques. The chart of accounts for the camping operation is provided below.

The General's Favorite Fishing Hole
Chart of Accounts

Assets
101   Cash
142   Office Supplies
144   Food Supplies
145   Prepaid Insurance
181   Fishing Boats
181.1 Accum. Depr.—Fishing Boats

Liabilities
202   Accounts Payable
219   Wages Payable

Owner's Equity
311   Bob Night, Capital
312   Bob Night, Drawing
313   Income Summary

Revenues
401   Registration Fees

Expenses
511   Wages Expense
521   Rent Expense
523   Office Supplies Expense
524   Food Supplies Expense
525   Telephone Expense
533   Utilities Expense
535   Insurance Expense
536   Postage Expense
542   Depr. Exp.—Fishing Boats

The following transactions took place during April 2000.

Apr. 1   Night invested cash in business, $90,000.

1   Paid insurance premium for camping season, $9,000.

2   Paid rent for lodge and campgrounds for the month of April, $40,000.

2   Deposited registration fees, $35,000.

2   Purchased ten fishing boats on account for $60,000. The boats have estimated useful lives of five years, at which time they will be donated to a local day camp. Arrangements were made to pay for the boats in July.

3   Purchased food supplies from Acme Super Market on account, $7,000.

5   Purchased office supplies from Gordon Office Supplies on account, $500.

7   Deposited registration fees, $38,600.

10   Purchased food supplies from Acme Super Market on account, $8,200.

10   Paid wages to fishing guides, $10,000.

14   Deposited registration fees, $30,500.

16   Purchased food supplies from Acme Super Market on account, $9,000.

17   Paid wages to fishing guides, $10,000.

18   Paid postage, $150.

21   Deposited registration fees, $35,600.

24   Purchased food supplies from Acme Super Market on account, $8,500.

24   Paid wages to fishing guides, $10,000.

28	Deposited registration fees, $32,000.
29	Paid wages to fishing guides, $10,000.
30	Purchased food supplies from Acme Super Market on account, $6,000.
30	Paid Acme Super Market on account, $32,700.
30	Paid utilities bill, $2,000.
30	Paid telephone bill, $1,200.
30	Bob Night withdrew cash for personal use, $6,000.

Adjustment information for the end of April is provided below.

(a) Office supplies remaining on hand, $100.

(b) Food supplies remaining on hand, $8,000.

(c) Insurance expired during the month of April, $1,500.

(d) Depreciation on the fishing boats for the month of April, $1,000.

(e) Wages earned, but not yet paid, at the end of April, $500.

Comprehensive Problem 1 involves processing the April transactions for The General's Favorite Fishing Hole, processing adjusting entries, generating financial statements, and changing the accounting period. Follow the steps below to complete the problem.

STEP 1: **Start up the QuickBooks software.**

Choose QuickBooks Pro from the Start button.

STEP 2: **Restore the Opening Balance data for Comprehensive Problem 1.**

▶ **From the File menu, choose Restore.**

▶ **When the Restore From window appears, select "Comprehensive Problem 1.QBB" and click on Open.**

▶ **When the Restore To window appears, use the Save in option to select the folder in which you wish to store your QuickBooks files, key a file name, and click on Save.**

The file name that you choose should identify the file as yours (C-1 Jane Doe). QuickBooks will add an extension of QBW.

▶ **If the file already exists, you will get a caution message. You must key "YES" and click OK to overwrite an existing file.**

STEP 3: **Enter the April transactions using the Make Journal Entry option.**

STEP 4: **Display the monthly transactions using the General Journal Report option from the Memorized Reports list.**

STEP 5: **If errors are detected on the Journal report, return to the General Journal entries screen and make corrections.**

STEP 6: **Display the Trial Balance Report from the Memorized Reports list.**

STEP 7: **Enter the adjusting entries for April 30, 2002 using the Make Journal Entry option. Key Adjusting Entry in the Memo field for each adjusting entry.**

STEP 8: **Display the adjusting entries using the General Journal Report option from the Memorized Reports list. The report will include monthly transactions plus adjusting entries.**

STEP 9: Display the Income Statement Report from the Memorized Reports list.

STEP 10: Display the Balance Sheet Report from the Memorized Reports list.

STEP 11: Display the Trial Balance Report from the Memorized Reports list.

STEP 12: Enter the closing entry to close the drawing account to capital on May 1, 2002.

STEP 13: Display the Post-Closing Trial Balance Report from the Memorized Reports list.

It isn't necessary to make closing entries to close out revenue and expense accounts. QuickBooks controls the process by date. Notice that the trial balance report as of May 1, 2002 (the beginning of a new fiscal period) has the revenue and expense accounts closed to Capital.

CHAPTER 7 DEMONSTRATION PROBLEM

Jason Kuhn's check stubs indicated a balance of $4,673.12 on March 31. This included a record of a deposit of $926.10 mailed to the bank on March 30 but not credited to Kuhn's account until April 1. In addition, the following checks were outstanding on March 31:

No. 462	$524.26
No. 465	$213.41
No. 473	$543.58
No. 476	$351.38
No. 477	$197.45

The bank statement showed a balance of $5,419.00 as of March 31. The bank statement included a service charge of $4.10 with the date of March 29. In matching the cancelled checks and record of deposits with the stubs, it was discovered that check no. 456, to Office Suppliers, Inc., for $93.00 was erroneously recorded on the stub for $39.00. This caused the bank balance on that stub and those following to be $54.00 too large. It was also discovered that an ATM withdrawal of $100.00 for personal use was not recorded on the books.

Kuhn maintains a $200.00 petty cash fund. His petty cash payments record showed the following totals at the end of March of the current year.

Automobile expense	$ 32.40
Postage expense	27.50
Charitable contributions expense	35.00
Telephone expense	6.20
Travel and entertainment expense	38.60
Miscellaneous expense	17.75
Jason Kuhn, Drawing	40.00
Total	$197.45

This left a balance of $2.55 in the petty cash fund.

Follow the steps below to complete the problem.

STEP 1: Start up the QuickBooks software.

Choose QuickBooks Pro from the Start button.

STEP 2: Restore the Opening Balance data for the Chapter 7 Demonstration Problem.

▶ From the File menu, choose Restore.

▶ When the Restore From window appears, select "07 Demonstration Problem.QBB" and click on Open.

▶ When the Restore To window appears, use the Save in option to select the folder in which you wish to store your QuickBooks files, key a file name, and click on Save.

The file name that you choose should identify the file as yours (07 Demo Jane Doe). QuickBooks will add an extension of QBW.

▶ If the file already exists, you will get a caution message. You must key "YES" and click OK to overwrite an existing file.

STEP 3: Key the journal entries to record the petty cash reimbursement and the entry to record the corrections detected on the statement. Key the entries in the Cash Journal. Do not include the service charge or interest earned in this journal entry because these items are entered as part of the reconciliation.

▶ From the Chart of Accounts list, double click the Cash account or click on the Activities button and select the Use Register option. The cash journal shown in Figure 2.8 will appear.

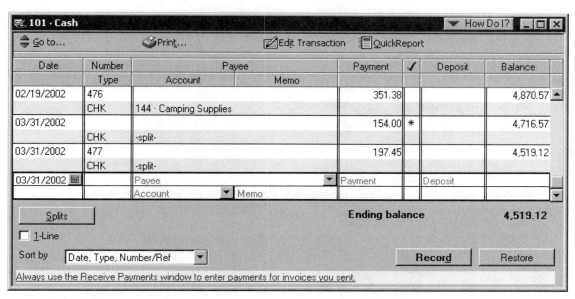

FIGURE 2.8 Cash Account Window

▶ For the petty cash reimbursement transaction, key as follows:

Key date of 03/31/02

Key the check number 477

Key the amount of the payment

Click on the Splits button

When the Split transaction window shown in Figure 2.9 appears, key each of the accounts and the amount for each account.

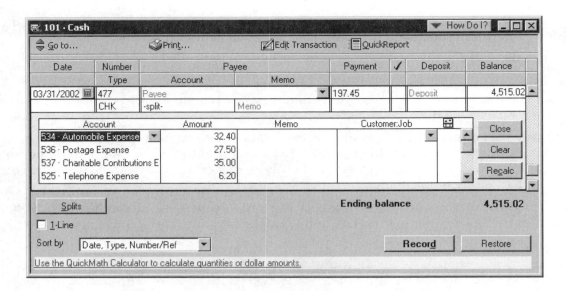

FIGURE 2.9 Split Transaction in the Cash Account Window

Click on Record

▶ **For the corrections transaction, key as follows:**

Key a date of 03/31/02

Key the total amount

Click on the Splits button

When the Split transaction window shown in Figure 2.10 appears, key each of the correction amounts.

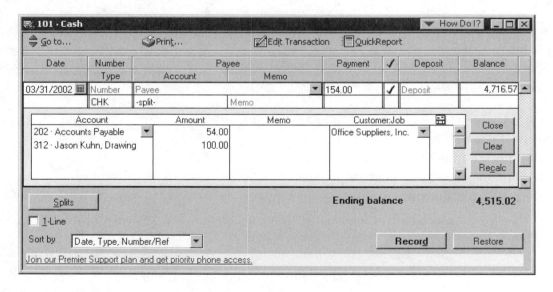

FIGURE 2.10 Split Transaction in the Cash Account Window

Click on Record

STEP 4:   From the Banking menu, choose the Reconcile option and reconcile the bank statement. The Reconcile window is shown in Figure 2.11.

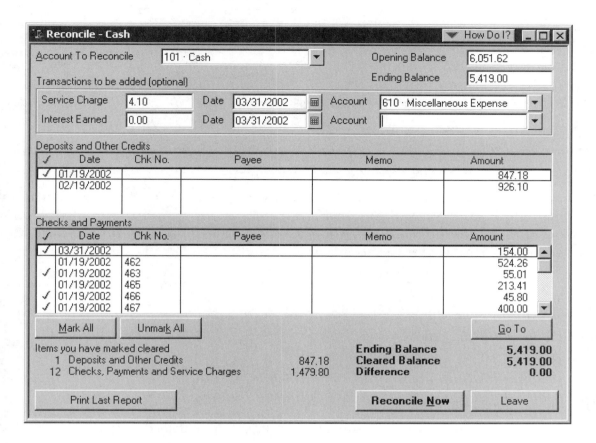

FIGURE 2.11 Reconcile–Cash Window

▶ Key the Bank Statement Balance into the Ending Balance field.

▶ Key the service charge with the date of 03/31/02 and choose the Miscellaneous Expense account.

▶ Click on the Mark All button.

▶ Click on the deposits that are outstanding. When finished all deposits with a check mark have cleared. Those without a check mark are outstanding.

▶ Select the checks that are outstanding. When finished all CLEARED checks should have a check mark. All outstanding checks should not.

▶ Verify that the fields near the bottom of the screen labeled Ending Balance and Cleared Balance are equal.

▶ Click on Reconcile Now. When asked for what type of report to print, select Summary. Key a Statement Closing Date of 03/31/02. Then, click OK.

STEP 5:   Display the journal entries using the Cash Journal Report option from the Memorized Reports list.

See the Solution section of this workbook for the solution to this demonstration problem.

PROBLEM 7-2A

The balance in the checking account of Lyle's Salon as of November 30 is $3,282.95. The bank statement shows an ending balance of $2,127.00. By examining last month's bank reconciliation, comparing the checks deposited and written per books and per bank in November, and noting the service charges and other debit and credit memos shown on the bank statement, the following were found:

(a) An ATM withdrawal of $150.00 on November 18 by Lyle for personal use was not recorded on the books.

(b) A bank debit memo issued for an NSFcheck from a customer of $19.50.

(c) A bank credit memo issued for interest of $19.00 earned during the month.

(d) On November 30, a deposit of $1,177.00 was made, which is not shown on the bank statement.

(e) A bank debit memo issued for $17.50 for bank service charges.

(f) Checks for the amounts of $185.00, $21.00, and $9.40 were written during November but have not yet been received by the bank.

(g) The reconciliation from the previous month showed outstanding checks of $271.95. One of those checks, for $18.65, has not yet been received by the bank.

(h) Check No. 523, written to a creditor in the amount of $372.90, was recorded in the books as $327.90.

Follow the steps below to complete the problem.

STEP 1:   **Start up the QuickBooks software.**

Choose QuickBooks Pro from the Start button.

STEP 2:   **Restore the Opening Balance data for Problem 7-2A.**

▶   **From the File menu, choose Restore.**

▶   **When the Restore From window appears, select "07-02A.QBB" and click on Open.**

▶   **When the Restore To window appears, use the Save in option to select the folder in which you wish to store your QuickBooks files, key a file name, and click on Save.**

The file name that you choose should identify the file as yours (07-02A Jane Doe). QuickBooks will add an extension of QBW.

▶   **If the file already exists, you will get a caution message. You must key "YES" and click OK to overwrite an existing file.**

STEP 3:   **Key the journal entries to record the items missing or in error from the bank statement. Key the entries in the Cash Journal. Do not include the service charge or interest earned in this journal entry because these items are entered as part of the reconciliation.**

▶   **From the Chart of Accounts list, double click the Cash account. The cash journal will appear.**

▶   **For each transaction key as follows:**
   Key date
   Key the check number (beginning with check number 531)
   Key the amount of the payment
   Click on the Splits button, if needed
   Key each of the accounts and the amount for each account
   Click on Record

STEP 4:   From the Banking menu, choose the Reconcile option and reconcile the bank statement.

▶   Key the Bank Statement Balance into the Ending Balance field.

▶   Key the service charge with the date of 11/30/02 and choose the Miscellaneous Expense account.

▶   Key the interest earned with the date of 11/30/02 and choose the Interest Earned account.

▶   Click on the Mark All button.

▶   Select the deposits that are outstanding.

▶   Select the checks that outstanding.

▶   Verify that the fields near the bottom of the screen labeled Ending Balance and Cleared Balance are equal.

▶   Click on Reconcile Now. When asked for what type of report to print, select Summary. Key a Statement Closing Date of 11/30/02. Then, click OK.

STEP 5:   Display the entries using the Cash Journal Report option from the Memorized Reports list.

PROBLEM 7-2B

The balance in the checking account of Tori's Health Center as of April 30 is $4,690.30. The bank statement shows an ending balance of $3,275.60. By examining last month's bank reconciliation, comparing the checks deposited and written per books and per bank in April, and noting the service charges and other debit and credit memos shown on the bank statement, the following were found:

(a) An ATM withdrawal of $200.00 on April 20 by Tori for personal use was not recorded on the books.

(b) A bank debit memo issued for an NSF check from a customer of $29.10.

(c) A bank credit memo issued for interest of $28.00 earned during the month.

(d) On April 30, a deposit of $1,592.00 was made, which is not shown on the bank statement.

(e) A bank debit memo issued for $24.50 for bank service charges.

(f)   Checks for the amounts of $215.00, $71.00, and $24.30 were written during April but have not yet been received by the bank.

(g) The reconciliation from the previous month showed outstanding checks of $418.25. One of these checks for $38.60 has not yet been received by the bank.

(h) Check No. 422, written to a creditor in the amount of $217.90, was recorded in the books as $271.90.

STEP 1:   Start up the QuickBooks software.

Choose QuickBooks Pro from the Start button.

STEP 2:   Restore the Opening Balance data for Problem 7-2B.

▶   From the File menu, choose Restore.

▶   When the Restore From window appears, select "07-02B.QBB" and click on Open.

▶   When the Restore To window appears, use the Save in option to select the folder in which you wish to store your QuickBooks files, key a file name, and click on Save.

The file name that you choose should identify the files as yours (07-02B Jane Doe). QuickBooks will add an extension of QBW.

▶ If the file already exists, you will get a caution message. You must key "YES" and click OK to overwrite an existing file.

STEP 3: Key the journal entries to record the items missing or in error from the bank statement. Key the entries in the Cash Journal. Click on the Splits button, if needed. Do not include the service charge or interest earned in the journal entry because these items are entered as part of the reconciliation. In the entry to correct item (h), key the amount in the deposit column rather than the payment column. Do not enter a check number for this entry.

▶ From the Chart of Accounts list, double click the Cash account. The cash journal will appear.

▶ For the remaining transaction key as follows:
Key date
Key the check number 428
Key the amount of the payment
Click on the Splits button
Key each of the accounts and the amount for each account
Click on Record

STEP 4: From the Banking menu, choose the Reconcile option and reconcile the bank statement.

▶ Key the Bank Statement Balance into the Ending Balance field.

▶ Key the service charge with the date of 04/30/02 and choose the Miscellaneous Expense account.

▶ Key the interest earned with the date of 04/30/02 and choose the Interest Earned account.

▶ Click on the Mark All button.

▶ Select the deposits that are outstanding.

▶ Select the checks that outstanding.

▶ Verify that the fields near the bottom of the screen labeled Ending Balance and Cleared Balance are equal.

▶ Click on Reconcile Now. When asked for what type of report to print, select Summary. Key a Statement Closing Date of 04/30/02. Then, click OK.

STEP 5: Display the entries using the Cash Journal Report from the Memorized Reports list.

CHAPTER 8 DEMONSTRATION PROBLEM

Carole Vohsen operates a pet grooming salon called Canine Coiffures. She has five employees, all of whom are paid on a weekly basis. Canine Coiffures uses a payroll register, individual employee earnings records, a journal, and a general ledger.

The payroll data for each employee for the week ended January 21, 2000, are given below. Employees are paid 1½ times the regular rate for work over 40 hours a week and double-time for work on Sunday.

Name	Employee No.	No. of Allowances	Marital Status	Total Hours Worked Jan. 15–21	Rate	Total Earnings Jan. 1–14
DeNourie, Katie	1	2	S	44	$11.50	$1,058.00
Garriott, Pete	2	1	M	40	12.00	1,032.00
Martinez, Sheila	3	3	M	39	12.50	987.50
Parker, Nancy	4	4	M	42	11.00	957.00
Shapiro, John	5	2	S	40	11.50	931.50

Sheila Martinez is the manager of the Shampooing Department. Her Social Security number is 500-88-4189, and she was born April 12, 1969. She lives at 46 Darling Crossing; Norwich, CT 06360. Martinez was hired September 1 of last year.

Social Security tax is withheld at the rate of 6.2% of the first $76,200 earned. Medicare tax is withheld at the rate of 1.45%, and city earnings tax at the rate of 1%, both applied to gross pay. The computer makes these calculations automatically. Garriott and Parker each have $14.00 and Denourie and Martinez each have $4.00 withheld for health insurance. DeNourie, Martinez, and Shapiro each have $15.00 withheld to be invested in the groomers' credit union. Garriott and Shapiro each have $18.75 withheld under a savings bond purchase plan.

Canine Coiffures' payroll is met by drawing checks on its regular bank account. This week, the checks were issued in sequence, beginning with no. 811.

The step-by-step instructions for completing the Chapter 8 Demonstration Problem are listed below.

STEP 1:   **Start up the QuickBooks software.**

Choose QuickBooks Pro from the Start button.

STEP 2:   **Restore the Opening Balance data for the Chapter 8 Demonstration Problem.**

▶ **From the File menu, choose Restore.**

▶ **When the Restore From window appears, select "08 Demonstration Problem.QBB" and click on Open.**

▶ **When the Restore To window appears, use the Save in option to select the folder in which you wish to store your QuickBooks files, key a file name, and click on Save.**

The file name that you choose should identify the file as yours (08 Demo Jane Doe). QuickBooks will add an extension of QBW.

▶ **If the file already exists, you will get a caution message. You must key "YES" and click OK to overwrite an existing file.**

STEP 3:   **From the Employees menu, choose the Pay Employees option.**

STEP 4:   **Key the Check Date to January 23, 2002 and the Payroll Period Ends date to January 21, 2002.**

STEP 5:   **Click on the Mark All button.**

STEP 6:   **Click the Create button to complete the payroll.**

Note: Click OK if a Warning appears on your screen. The results of Steps 3–6 are shown in Figure 2.12.

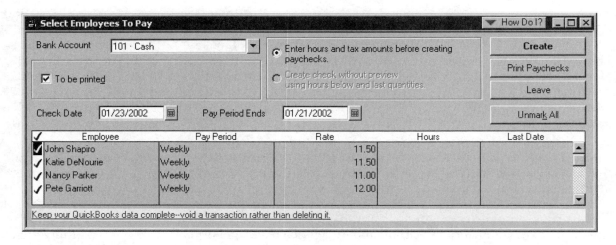

FIGURE 2.12 Select Employees To Pay Window

STEP 7: **When the Preview Paycheck screen appears, very carefully enter the following for each employee:**

Regular and overtime hours.

Under Employee Summary, enter the Federal Withholding, Social Security, and Medicare.

Under Company Summary, enter the Social Security and Medicare amounts.

Click on the Create button. Once the paycheck is created, it may not be changed.

Note: Although QuickBooks is capable of calculating federal withholding, social security, and medicare taxes, it cannot do so unless you are a subscriber to their tax service. If you are not a subscriber, you will need to look up the Federal Withholding in a Wage-Bracket withholding table, calculate the Social Security and Medicare taxes, and key them. The 1% city tax is automatically calculated by the computer. The information for John Shapiro is previewed in Figure 2.13.

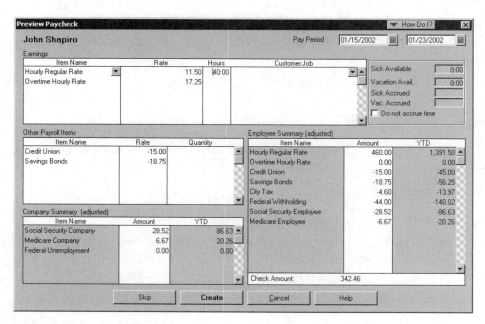

FIGURE 2.13 Preview Paycheck Window

STEP 8: From the Memorized Reports list, display the following reports:

Payroll Summary Report

Payroll Liabilities Report

Payroll Journal Entries Report

See the Solution section of this workbook for the solution to this demonstration problem.

PROBLEM 8-2A

Don McCullum operates a travel agency called Don's Luxury Travel. He has five employees, all of whom are paid on a weekly basis. The travel agency uses a payroll register, individual employee earnings records, and a general journal.

Don's Luxury Travel uses a weekly federal income tax withholding table. The payroll data for each employee for the week ended March 22, 2000, are given below. Employees are paid 1½ times the regular rate for working over 40 hours per week.

Name	No. of Allowances	Marital Status	Total Hours Worked Mar. 16–22	Rate	Total Earnings Jan. 1–Mar. 15
Ali, Loren	4	M	45	$11.00	$5,280.00
Carson, Judy	1	S	40	12.00	5,760.00
Hernandez, Maria	3	M	43	9.50	4,560.00
Knox, Wayne	1	S	39	11.00	5,125.50
Paglione, Jim	2	M	40	10.50	4,720.50

Social Security tax is withheld from the first $76,200 of earnings at the rate of 6.2%. Medicare tax is withheld at the rate of 1.45%, and city earnings tax at the rate of 1%, both applied to gross pay. The computer makes these calculations automatically. Ali and Knox have $15.00 withheld and Carson and Hernandez have $5.00 withheld for health insurance. Ali and Knox have $20.00 withheld to be invested in the travel agencies' credit union. Carson has $38.75 withheld and Hernandez has $18.75 withheld under a savings bond purchase plan.

Don's Luxury Travel's payroll is met by drawing checks on its regular bank account. The checks were issued in sequence, beginning with check no. 423.

The step-by-step instructions for completing Problem 8-2A are listed below.

STEP 1: **Start up the QuickBooks software.**

Choose QuickBooks Pro from the Start button.

STEP 2: **Restore the Opening Balance data for Problem 8-2A.**

▶ **From the File menu, choose Restore.**

▶ **When the Restore From window appears, select "08-02A.QBB" and click on Open.**

▶ **When the Restore To window appears, use the Save in option to select the folder in which you wish to store your QuickBooks files, key a file name, and click on Save.**

The file name you choose should identify the file as yours (08-02A Jane Doe). QuickBooks will add an extension of QBW.

▶ **If the file already exists, you will get a caution message. You must key "YES" and click OK to overwrite an existing file.**

STEP 3: **From the Employees menu, choose the Pay Employees option.**

STEP 4:   Key the Check Date to March 24, 2002 and the Payroll Period Ends date to April 22, 2002.

STEP 5:   Click on the Mark All button.

STEP 6:   Click the Create button to complete the payroll.

Note: Click OK if a Warning appears on your screen.

STEP 7:   When the Preview Paycheck screen appears, very carefully enter the following for each employee:

Regular and overtime hours.

Under Employee Summary, enter the Federal Withholding, Social Security, and Medicare.

Under Company Summary, enter the Social Security and Medicare amounts.

Click on the Create button. Once the paycheck is created, it may not be changed.

Note: Although QuickBooks is capable of calculating federal withholding, social security, and medicare taxes, it cannot do so unless you are a subscriber to their tax service. If you are not a subscriber, you will need to look up the Federal Withholding in a Wage-Bracket withholding table, calculate the Social Security and Medicare taxes, and key them. The 1% city tax is automatically calculated by the computer.

STEP 8:   From the Memorized Reports list, display the following reports:

Payroll Summary Report

Payroll Liabilities Report

Payroll Journal Entries Report

Trial Balance Report

PROBLEM 8-2B

Karen Jolly operates a bakery called Karen's Cupcakes. She has five employees, all of whom are paid on a weekly basis. Karen's Cupcakes uses a payroll register, individual employee earnings records, and a general journal. The payroll data for each employee for the week ended February 15, 2000, are given below. Employees are paid 1½ times the regular rate for working over 40 hours per week.

Name	No. of Allowances	Marital Status	Total Hours Worked Feb. 9–15	Rate	Total Earnings Jan. 1–Feb. 15
Barone, William	1	S	40	$10.00	$2,400.00
Hastings, Gene	4	M	45	12.00	3,360.00
Nitobe, Isako	3	M	46	8.75	2,935.00
Smith, Judy	4	M	42	11.00	2,745.00
Tarshis, Dolores	1	S	39	10.50	2,650.75

Social Security tax is withheld from the first $76,200 of earnings at the rate of 6.2%. Medicare tax is withheld at the rate of 1.45%, and city earnings tax at the rate of 1%, both applied to gross pay. Withholding tax calculations are made automatically by the computer. Hastings and Smith have $35.00 withheld and Nitobe and Tarshis have $15.00 withheld for health insurance. Nitobe and Tarshis have $25.00 withheld to be invested in the bakers' credit union. Hastings has $18.75 withheld and Smith has $43.75 withheld under a savings bond purchase plan.

Karen's Cupcakes' payroll is met by drawing checks on its regular bank account. The checks were issued in sequence, beginning with no. 365.

The step-by-step instructions for completing Problem 8-2B are listed below.

STEP 1:   Start up the QuickBooks software.

Choose QuickBooks Pro from the Start button.

STEP 2:   Restore the Opening Balance data for Problem 8-2B.

▶ **From the File menu, choose Restore.**

▶ **When the Restore From window appears, select "08-02B.QBB" and click on Open.**

▶ **When the Restore To window appears, use the Save in option to select the folder in which you wish to store your QuickBooks files, key a file name, and click on Save.**

The file name that you choose should identify the file as yours (08-02B Jane Doe). QuickBooks will add an extension of QBW.

▶ **If the file already exists, you will get a caution message. You must key "YES" and click OK to overwrite an existing file.**

STEP 3:   From the Employees menu, choose the Pay Employees option.

STEP 4:   Key the Check Date to February 17, 2002 and the Payroll Period Ends date to February 15, 2002.

STEP 5:   Click on the Mark All button.

STEP 6:   Click the Create button to complete the payroll.

Note: Click OK if a Warning appears on your screen.

STEP 7:   When the Preview Paycheck screen appears, very carefully enter the following for each employee:

Regular and overtime hours.

Under Employee Summary, enter the Federal Withholding, Social Security, and Medicare.

Under Company Summary, enter the Social Security and Medicare amounts.

Click on the Create button. Once the paycheck is created, it may not be changed.

Note: Although QuickBooks is capable of calculating federal withholding, social security, and medicare taxes, it cannot do so unless you are a subscriber to their tax service. If you are not a subscriber, you will need to look up the Federal Withholding in a Wage-Bracket withholding table, calculate the Social Security and Medicare taxes, and key them. The 1% city tax is automatically calculated by the computer.

STEP 8:   From the Memorized Reports list, display the following reports:

Payroll Summary Report

Payroll Liabilities Report

Payroll Journal Entries Report

Trial Balance Report

CHAPTER 8 MASTERY PROBLEM

Abigail Trenkamp owns and operates the Trenkamp Collection Agency. Listed below are the name, number of allowances claimed, marital status, information from time cards on hours worked each day, and the hourly rate of each employee. All hours worked in excess of 40 hours for Monday through Friday are paid at 1½ times the regular rate. All weekend hours are paid at double the regular rate.

Social Security tax is withheld at the rate of 6.2% for the first $76,200 earned. Medicare tax is withheld at 1.45% and state income tax at 3.5%. Each employee has $5.00 withheld for health insurance. All employees use payroll deduction to the credit union for varying amounts as listed on the next page.

Trenkamp Collection Agency
Payroll Information for the Week Ended November 18, 2000

| Name | Employee No. | No. of Allow. | Marital Status | Regular Hours Worked | | | | | | | Hourly Rate | Credit Union Deposit | Total Earnings 1/1–11/11 |
				S	S	M	T	W	T	F			
Berling, James	1	3	M	2	2	9	8	8	9	10	$12.00	$149.60	$24,525.00
Merz, Linda	2	4	M	4	3	8	8	8	8	11	10.00	117.00	20,480.00
Goetz, Ken	3	5	M	0	0	6	7	8	9	10	11.00	91.30	21,500.00
Menick, Judd	4	2	M	8	8	0	0	8	8	9	11.00	126.50	22,625.00
Morales, Eva	5	3	M	0	0	8	8	8	6	8	13.00	117.05	24,730.00
Heimbrock, Jacob	6	2	S	0	0	8	8	8	8	8	30.00	154.25	67,600.00
Townsley, Sarah	7	2	M	4	0	6	6	6	6	4	9.00	83.05	21,425.00
Salzman, Ben	8	4	M	6	2	8	8	6	6	6	11.00	130.00	6,635.00
Layton, Esther	9	4	M	0	0	8	8	8	8	8	11.00	88.00	5,635.00
Thompson, David	10	5	M	0	2	10	9	7	7	10	11.00	128.90	21,635.00
Vadillo, Carmen	11	2	S	8	0	4	8	8	8	9	13.00	139.11	24,115.00

The Trenkamp Collection Agency follows the practice of drawing a single check for the net amount of the payroll and depositing the check in a special payroll account at the bank. Individual checks issued were numbered consecutively, beginning with no. 331.

In the Chapter 8 Mastery Problem, you will process the payroll for the week ended November 18, 2000, for Trenkamp Collection. The step-by-step instructions for completing the Problem are listed below.

STEP 1:   Start up the QuickBooks software.

Choose QuickBooks Pro from the Start button.

STEP 2:   Restore the Opening Balance data for the Chapter 8 Mastery Problem.

► **From the File menu, choose Restore.**

► **When the Restore From window appears, select "08 Mastery Problem.QBB" and click on Open.**

► **When the Restore To window appears, use the Save in option to select the folder in which you wish to store your QuickBooks files, key a file name, and click on Save.**

The file name that you choose should identify the file as yours (08 Mastery Jane Doe). QuickBooks will add an extension of QBW.

► **If the file already exists, you will get a caution message. You must key "YES" and click OK to overwrite an existing file.**

STEP 3: From the Employees menu, choose the Pay Employees option.

STEP 4: Key the Check Date to November 21, 2002 and the Payroll Period Ends date to November 18, 2002.

STEP 5: Click on the Mark All button.

STEP 6: Click the Create button to complete the payroll.

STEP 7: When the Preview Paycheck screen appears, very carefully enter the following:

Regular, overtime and double-time hours.

Under Employee Summary, enter the Federal Withholding, Social Security, and Medicare.

Under Company Summary, enter the Social Security and Medicare amounts.

Click on the Create button. Once the paycheck is created, it may not be changed.

Note: Although QuickBooks is capable of calculating federal withholding, social security, and medicare taxes, it cannot do so unless you are a subscriber to their tax service. If you are not a subscriber, you will need to look up the Federal Withholding in a Wage-Bracket withholding table, calculate the Social Security and Medicare taxes, and key them.

STEP 8: From the Memorized Reports list, display the following reports:

Payroll Summary Report

Payroll Liabilities Report

Payroll Journal Entries Report

CHAPTER 9 DEMONSTRATION PROBLEM

The totals from Hart Company's payroll register for the week ended December 31, 2000, is as follows:
    Total earnings, $3,800
    Taxable Earnings:
        Unemployment compensation, $400
        Social Securioty, $3,800
    Federal Income Tax, $380
    Social Security Tax, $235.60
    Medicare Tax, $55.10
    Health Insurance, $50.00
    United Way, $100
Net Pay, $2,979.30
Payroll taxes are imposed as follows: Social Security, 6.2%; Medicare, 1.45%; FUTA, 0.8%; and SUTA, 5.4%.

REQUIRED
1. a. Prepare the journal entry for payment of this payroll on December 31, 2000.

b. Prepare the journal entry for the employer's payroll taxes for the period ended December 31, 2000.

2. Hart Company had the following balances in its general ledger after the entries for Requirement 1 were made:

Employee Income Tax Payable	$1,520.00
Social Security Tax Payable	1,847.00
Medicare Tax Payable	433.00
FUTA Tax Payable	27.20
SUTA Tax Payable	183.60

a.   Prepare the journal entry for payment of the liabilities for employee federal income taxes and Social Security and Medicare taxes on January 15, 2000.

        b. Prepare the journal entry for payment of the liability for FUTA tax on January 31, 2000

        c. Prepare the journal entry for payment of the liability for SUTA tax on January 31, 2000.

    3.   Hart Company paid a premium of $280 for workers' compensation insurance based on estimated payroll as of the beginning of the year. Based on actual payroll as of the end of the year, the premium is $298. Prepare the adjusting entry to reflect the underpayment of the insurance premium.

In the Chapter 9 Demonstration Problem you will enter the journal entries to record the payroll, the employer's payroll taxes, and the payment of payroll withholding liabilities. Follow the steps listed to complete the Chapter 9 Demonstration Problem.

STEP 1:   **Start up the QuickBooks software.**

Choose QuickBooks Pro from the Start button.

STEP 2:   **Restore the Opening Balance data for the Chapter 9 Demonstration Problem.**

▶ **From the File menu, choose Restore.**

▶ **When the Restore From window appears, select "09 Demonstration Problem.QBB" and click on Open.**

▶ **When the Restore To window appears, use the Save in option to select the folder in which you wish to store your QuickBooks files, key a file name, and click on Save.**

The file name you choose should identify the file as yours (09 Demo Jane Doe). QuickBooks will add an extension of QBW.

▶ **If the file already exists, you will get a caution message. You must key "YES" and click OK to overwrite an existing file.**

STEP 3:   **From the Company menu, choose the Make Journal Entry option and key the general journal entry to record the payment of payroll.**

STEP 4   **Make the journal entry to record the payment of the employer's payroll taxes for December 31, 2002**

STEP 5:   **Display the journal entries using the December Journal Report from the Memorized Reports list. The December Journal Report for the Hart Company is shown in Figure 2.14.**

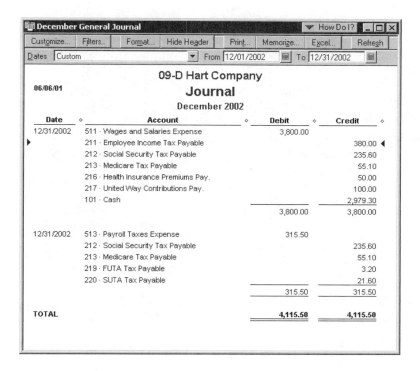

FIGURE 2.14 December General Journal Window

STEP 6: Key the general journal entry to record the payment of the employee federal income tax, social security tax, and Medicare tax on January 15, 2003.

STEP 7: Key the general journal entry to record payment of the FUTA tax and the entry to record the SUTA tax on January 31, 2003.

STEP 8: Key the adjusting entry to record the underpayment of the workers' compensation insurance premium on January 31, 2003.

STEP 9: Display the January Journal Report from the Memorized Reports list.

See the Solution section of this workbook for the solution to this demonstration problem.

PROBLEM 9-2A

The Cascade Company has four employees. All are paid on a monthly basis. The fiscal year of the business is July 1 to June 30. Payroll taxes are imposed as follows:

1. Social Security tax of 6.2% withheld from employees' wages on the first $76,200 of earnings and Medicare tax withheld at 1.45% of gross earnings.

2. Social Security tax of 6.2% imposed on the employer on the first $76,200 of earnings and Medicare tax of 1.45% on gross earnings.

3. SUTA tax of 5.4% imposed on the employer on the first $7,000 of earnings.

4. FUTA tax of 0.8% imposed on the employer on the first $7,000 of earnings.

The accounts kept by Cascade include the following:

Account Number	Title	Balance on July 1
101	Cash	$50,200
211	Employee Income Tax Payable	1,015
212	Social Security Tax Payable	1,458
213	Medicare Tax Payable	342
218	Savings Bond Deductions Payable	350
221	FUTA Tax Payable	164
222	SUTA Tax Payable	810
511	Wages and Salaries Expense	0
530	Payroll Taxes Expense	0

The following transactions relating to payrolls and payroll taxes occurred during July and August.

July 15 Paid $2,815 covering the following June taxes:

Social Security tax	$ 1,458
Medicare tax	342
Employee income tax withheld	1,015
Total	$ 2,815

31 July payroll:

Total wages and salaries expense		$12,000
Less amounts withheld:		
Social Security tax	$ 744	
Medicare tax	174	
Employee income tax	1,020	
Savings bond deductions	350	2,288
Net amount paid		$ 9,712

31 Purchased savings bonds for employees, $700

31 Data for completing employer's payroll taxes expense for July:

Social Security taxable wages	$12,000
Unemployment taxable wages	3,000

Aug. 15 Paid $2,856 covering the following July taxes:

Social Security tax	$ 1,488
Medicare tax	348
Employee income tax withheld	1,020
Total	$ 2,856

15 Paid SUTA tax for the quarter, $972

15 Paid FUTA tax, $188

In Problem 9-2A, you will enter the journal entries to record the payroll, the employer's payroll taxes, and the payment of payroll withholding liabilities. Follow the steps listed to complete the Problem 9-2A.

STEP 1: Start up the QuickBooks software.

Choose QuickBooks Pro from the Start button.

STEP 2: Restore the Opening Balance data for Problem 9-2A.

▶ **From the File menu, choose Restore.**

▶ **When the Restore From window appears, select "09-02A.QBB" and click on Open.**

- ▶ When the Restore To window appears, use the Save in option to select the folder in which you wish to store your QuickBooks files, key a file name, and click on Save.

  The file name that you choose should identify the file as yours (09-02A Jane Doe). QuickBooks will add an extension of QBW.

- ▶ If the file already exists, you will get a caution message. You must key "YES" and click OK to overwrite an existing file.

STEP 3: From the Company menu, choose the Make Journal Entry option and key the journal entries to record the payroll taxes for July and August of 2002.

STEP 4: Display the Journal Report for July and August 2002 from the Memorized Reports list.

PROBLEM 9-2B

The Oxford Company has five employees. All are paid on a monthly basis. The fiscal year of the business is June 1 to May 31. Payroll taxes are imposed as follows:

1. Social Security tax of 6.2% to be withheld from employees' wages on the first $76,200 of earnings and Medicare tax of 1.45% on gross earnings.

2. Social Security tax of 6.2% imposed on the employer on the first $76,200 of earnings and Medicare tax of 1.45% on gross earnings.

3. SUTA tax of 5.4% imposed on the employer on the first $7,000 of earnings.

4. FUTA tax of 0.8% imposed on the employer on the first $7,000 of earnings.

The accounts kept by the Oxford Company include the following:

Account Number	Title	Balance on June 1
101	Cash	$48,650
211	Employee Income Tax Payable	1,345
212	Social Security Tax Payable	1,823
213	Medicare Tax Payable	427
218	Savings Bond Deductions Payable	525
221	FUTA Tax Payable	360
222	SUTA Tax Payable	920
511	Wages and Salaries Expense	0
530	Payroll Taxes Expense	0

The following transactions relating to payrolls and payroll taxes occurred during June and July.

June 15	Paid $3,595.00 covering the following May taxes:	
	Social Security tax	$ 1,823.00
	Medicare tax	427.00
	Employee income tax withheld	1,345.00
	Total	$ 3,595.00

30	June payroll:		
	Total wages and salaries expense		$14,700.00
	Less amounts withheld:		
	Social Security tax	$ 911.40	
	Medicare tax	213.15	
	Employee income tax	1,280.00	
	Savings bond deductions	525.00	2,929.55
	Net amount paid		$11,770.45

30 Purchased savings bonds for employees, $1,050.00

30	Data for completing employer's payroll taxes expense for June:	
	Social Security taxable wages	$14,700.00
	Unemployment taxable wages	4,500.00

July 15	Paid $3,529.10 covering the following June taxes:	
	Social Security tax	$ 1,822.80
	Medicare tax	426.30
	Employee income tax withheld	1,280.00
	Total	$ 3,529.10

15 Paid SUTA tax for the quarter, $1,163.00

15 Paid FUTA tax, $396.00

In Problem 9-2B, you will enter the journal entries to record the payroll, the employer's payroll taxes, and the payment of payroll withholding liabilities. Follow the steps listed to complete the problem.

STEP 1:   Start up the QuickBooks software.

Choose QuickBooks Pro from the Start button.

STEP 2:   Restore the Opening Balance data for Problem 9-2B.

▶ **From the File menu, choose Restore.**

▶ **When the Restore From window appears, select "09-02B.QBB" and click on Open.**

▶ **When the Restore To window appears, use the Save in option to select the folder in which you wish to store your QuickBooks files, key a file name, and click on Save.**

The file name that you choose should identify the file as yours (09-02B Jane Doe). QuickBooks will add an extension of QBW.

▶ **If the file already exists, you will get a caution message. You must key "YES" and click OK to overwrite an existing file.**

STEP 3:   From the Company menu, choose the Make Journal Entry option and key the journal entries to record the payroll taxes for June and July of 2002.

STEP 4:   Display the Journal Report for June and July 2002 from the Memorized Reports list.

CHAPTER 9 MASTERY PROBLEM

The totals from Nix Company's payroll register for the week ended March 31, 2000 is as follows:

Earnings, $5500
Taxable Earnings:
    Unemployment compensation, $5,000
    Social Security, $5,500
Federal Income Tax, $500
Social Security Tax, $341
Medicare Tax, $79.75

Health Insurance, $165
Life Insurance, $200
Net Pay, $4,214.25

Payroll taxes are imposed as follows:Social Security tax, 6.2%; Medicare tax, 1.45%; FUTA tax, 0.8%; and SUTA tax, 5.4%.

REQUIRED
1. a. Prepare the journal entry for payment of this payroll on March 31, 2000.

   b. Prepare the journal entry for the employer's payroll taxes for the period ended March 31, 2000.

2. Nix Company had the following balances in its general ledger before the entries for Requirement 1 were made:

Employee income tax payable	$2,500
Social Security tax payable	2,008
Medicare tax payable	470
FUTA tax payable	520
SUTA tax payable	3,510

   a. Prepare the journal entry for payment of the liabilities for federal income taxes and Social Security and Medicare taxes on April 15, 2000.

   b. Prepare the journal entry for payment of the liability for FUTA tax on April 30, 2000.

   c. Prepare the journal entry for payment of the liability for SUTA tax on April 30, 2000.

3. Nix Company paid a premium of $420 for workers' compensation insurance based on the estimated payroll as of the beginning of the year. Based on actual payroll as of the end of the year, the premium is only $400. Prepare the adjusting entry to reflect the overpayment of the insurance premium at the end of the year (December 31, 2000).

In the Chapter 9 Mastery Problem, you will enter the journal entries to record the payroll, the employer's payroll taxes, and the payment of payroll withholding liabilities. Follow the steps listed below to complete the problem.

STEP 1: Start up the QuickBooks software.

Choose QuickBooks Pro from the Start button.

STEP 2: Restore the Opening Balance data for the Chapter 9 Mastery Problem.

▶ **From the File menu, choose Restore.**

▶ **When the Restore From window appears, select "09 Mastery Problem.QBB" and click on Open.**

▶ **When the Restore To window appears, use the Save in option to select the folder in which you wish to store your QuickBooks files, key a file name, and click on Save.**

The file name that you choose should identify the file as yours (09 Mastery Jane Doe). QuickBooks will add an extension of QBW.

▶ **If the file already exists, you will get a caution message. You must key "YES" and click OK to overwrite an existing file.**

STEP 3: From the Company menu, choose the Make Journal Entry option and key the general journal entry to record the payment of payroll and the entry to record the payment of the employer's payroll taxes for March 31, 2002.

STEP 4: Display the journal entries using the March Journal Report from the Memorized Reports list.

STEP 5: Key the general journal entry to record the payment of the employee federal income tax, social security tax, and Medicare tax on April 15, 2002.

STEP 6: Key the general journal entry to record payment of the FUTA tax and the entry to record the SUTA tax on April 30, 2002.

STEP 7: Display the April Journal Report from the Memorized Reports list.

STEP 8: Key the adjusting entry to record the overpayment of the workers' compensation insurance premium on December 31, 2002.

STEP 9: Display the December Journal Report from the Memorized Reports list.

CHAPTER 10 DEMONSTRATION PROBLEM

Maria Vietor is a financial planning consultant. She developed the following chart of accounts for her business.

Vietor Financial Planning
Chart of Accounts

Assets
101   Cash
142   Office Supplies

Liabilities
202   Accounts Payable

Owner's Equity
311   Maria Vietor, Capital
312   Maria Vietor, Drawing
313   Income Summary

Revenues
401   Professional Fees

Expenses
511   Wages Expense
521   Rent Expense
523   Office Supplies Expense
525   Telephone Expense
526   Automobile Expense
533   Utilities Expense
534   Charitable Contributions Expense

Vietor completed the following transactions during the month of December of the current year:

Dec. 1   Vietor invested cash to start a consulting business, $20,000.

3   Paid December office rent, $1,000.

4   Received a check from Aaron Bisno, a client, for services, $2,500.

6   Paid Union Electric for December heating and light, $75.

7   Received a check from Will Carter, a client, for services, $2,000.

12   Paid Smith's Super Service for gasoline and oil purchases, $60.

14   Paid Comphelp for temporary secretarial services obtained through them during the past two weeks, $600.

17   Purchased office supplies on account from Cleat Office Supply, $280.

20   Paid Cress Telephone Co. for local and long-distance business calls during the past month, $100.

21   Vietor withdrew cash for personal use, $1,100.

24   Made donation to the National Multiple Sclerosis Society, $100.

27   Received a check from Ellen Thaler, a client, for services, $2,000.

28   Paid Comphelp for temporary secretarial services obtained through them during the past two weeks, $600.

29   Made payment on account to Cleat Office Supply, $100.

Follow the step-by-step instructions below to complete the problem.

STEP 1:   **Start up the QuickBooks software.**

Choose QuickBooks Pro from the Start button.

STEP 2:   **Restore the Opening Balance data for the Chapter 10 Demonstration Problem.**

▶ **From the File menu, choose Restore.**

▶ **When the Restore From window appears, select "10 Demonstration Problem.QBB" and click on Open.**

▶ **When the Restore To window appears, use the Save in option to select the folder in which you wish to store your QuickBooks files, key a file name, and click on Save.**

The file name that you choose should identify the file as yours (10 Demo Jane Doe). QuickBooks will add an extension of QBW.

▶ **If the file already exists, you will get a caution message. You must key "YES" and click OK to overwrite an existing file.**

STEP 3:   **From the Company menu, choose the Make Journal Entry option and key the transactions for December, 2002. The first journal entry is illustrated in the General Journal Entry window shown in Figure 2.15**

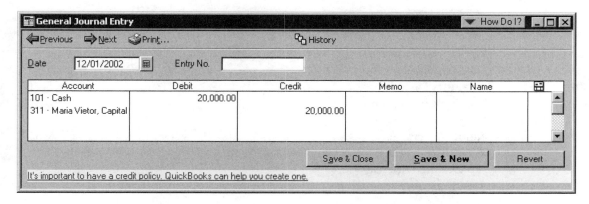

FIGURE 2.15 General Journal Entry Window

Note: If the transaction involves accounts payable, you must enter or select from the drop list in the Name field, the vendor name. An entry involving Accounts Payable is illustrated in Figure 2.16.

FIGURE 2.16 Accounts Payable Entry in the General Journal Entry Window

STEP 4:   Display the Journal Report from the Memorized Reports list.

STEP 5:   Display the General Ledger Report from the Memorized Reports list.

STEP 6:   Display the Trial Balance Report from the Memorized Reports list.

See the Solution section of this workbook for the solution to this demonstration problem.

PROBLEM 10-2A

Sue Reyton owns a suit tailoring shop. She opened her business in September. She rents a small work space and has an assistant to receive job orders and process claim tickets. Her trial balance on the next page shows her account balances for the first two months of business (September and October). No adjustments were made in September or October.

Sue Reyton Tailors
Trial Balance
As Of 10/31/00

Acct. Number	Account Title	Debit	Credit
101	Cash	5711.00	
141	Tailoring Supplies	1000.00	
142	Office Supplies	485.00	
145	Prepaid Insurance	100.00	
188	Tailoring Equipment	3800.00	
202	Accounts Payable		4125.00
311	Sue Reyton, Capital		5430.00
312	Sue Reyton, Drawing	500.00	
401	Tailoring Fees		3600.00
511	Wages Expense	800.00	
512	Advertising Expense 3	3.00	
521	Rent Expense	600.00	
525	Telephone Expense	60.00	
533	Electricity Expense	44.00	
549	Miscellaneous Expense	22.00	
	Totals	13155.00	13155.00

Reyton's transactions for November are as follows:

Nov. 1   Paid November rent, $300.

2   Purchased tailoring supplies on account from Sew Easy Supplies, $150.

3   Purchased a new buttonhole machine on account from Seam's Sewing Machines, $3,000.

5   Earned first week's revenue: $400 in cash.

8   Paid for newspaper advertising, $13.

9   Paid telephone bill, $28.

10   Paid electricity bill, $21.

12   Earned second week's revenue: $200 in cash, $300 on account.

15   Paid part-time worker, $400.

16   Made payment on account for tailoring supplies, $100.

17   Paid for magazine subscription (miscellaneous expense), $12.

19	Earned third week's revenue: $450 in cash.
21	Paid for prepaid insurance for the year, $500.
23	Received cash from customers (previously owed), $300.
24	Paid for newspaper advertising, $13.
26	Paid for special delivery fee (miscellaneous expense), $12.
29	Earned fourth week's revenue: $600 in cash.

Additional accounts needed are as follows:

Nov. 30 Adjustments:

(a) Tailoring supplies on hand, $450.

(b) Office supplies on hand, $285.

(c) Prepaid insurance expired over past three months, $150.

(d) Depreciation on tailoring equipment for the last three months, $300.

Problem 10-2A involves entering the November transactions for Sue Reyton Tailors in the general journal, processing adjusting entries, generating financial statements, and changing the accounting period.

Follow the step-by-step instructions below to complete the problem.

STEP 1: **Start up the QuickBooks software.**

Choose QuickBooks Pro from the Start button.

STEP 2: **Restore the Opening Balance data for Problem 10-2A.**

▶ **From the File menu, choose Restore.**

▶ **When the Restore From window appears, select "10-2A.QBB" and click on Open.**

▶ **When the Restore To window appears, use the Save in option to select the folder in which you wish to store your QuickBooks files, key a file name, and click on Save.**

The file name that you choose should identify the file as yours (10-02A Jane Doe). QuickBooks will add an extension of QBW.

▶ **If the file already exists, you will get a caution message. You must key "YES" and click OK to overwrite an existing file.**

STEP 3: **From the Company menu, choose the Make Journal Entry option and key the transactions for November, 2002.**

Note: If the transaction involves accounts payable, you must enter or select from the drop list in the Name field, the vendor name.

STEP 4: **Display the November Journal Report from the Memorized Reports list.**

STEP 5: **Display the Trial Balance Report from the Memorized Reports list.**

STEP 6: **Enter the adjusting entries for November 30, 2002 using the Make Journal Entry option. Key Adjusting Entry in the Memo field for each adjusting entry.**

STEP 7: **Display the adjusting entries using the Adjusting Entries Journal Report option from the Memorized Reports list.**

STEP 8: **Display the Income Statement Report from the Memorized Reports list.**

STEP 9: Display the Balance Sheet Report from the Memorized Reports list.

STEP 10: Enter the closing entry to close the drawing account to capital on December 1, 2002.

STEP 11: Display the Post-Closing Trial Balance Report from the Memorized Reports list.

It isn't necessary to make closing entries to close out revenue and expense accounts. QuickBooks controls the process by date. Notice that the trial balance report as of December 1, 2002 (the beginning of a new fiscal period) has the revenue and expense accounts closed to Capital.

PROBLEM 10-2B

Molly Claussen owns a lawn care business. She opened her business in April. She rents a small shop area where she stores her equipment and has an assistant to receive orders and process accounts. Her trial balance shows her account balances for the first two months of business (April and May). No adjustments were made at the end of April or May.

Claussen's Green Thumb
Trial Balance
As Of 06/30/00

Acct. Number	Account Title	Debit	Credit
101	Cash	4604.00	
141	Lawn Care Supplies	588.00	
142	Office Supplies	243.00	
145	Prepaid Insurance	150.00	
189	Lawn Care Equipment	2408.00	
202	Accounts Payable		1080.00
311	Molly Claussen, Capital		5000.00
312	Molly Claussen, Drawing	800.00	
401	Lawn Care Fees		4033.00
511	Wages Expense	600.00	
521	Rent Expense	400.00	
525	Telephone Expense	88.00	
533	Electricity Expense	62.00	
537	Repair Expense	50.00	
538	Gas and Oil Expense	120.00	
	Totals	10113.00	10113.00

Transactions for June are as follows:

June 1   Paid shop rent, $200.

    2   Purchased office supplies, $230.

    3   Purchased new landscaping equipment on account from Earth Care, Inc., $1,000.

    5   Paid telephone bill, $31.

    6   Received cash for lawn care fees, $640.

    8   Paid electricity bill, $31.

   10   Paid part-time worker, $300.

   11   Received cash for lawn care fees, $580.

12	Paid for a one-year insurance policy, $200.
14	Made payment on account for landscaping equipment previously purchased, $100.
15	Paid for gas and oil, $40.
19	Paid for mower repairs, $25.
21	Received $310 cash for lawn care fees and earned $480 on account.
24	Withdrew cash for personal use, $100.
26	Paid for edging equipment repairs, $20.
28	Received cash from customers (previously owed), $480.
29	Paid part-time worker, $300.

June 30 Adjustments:

(a) Office supplies on hand, $273.

(b) Lawn care supplies on hand, $300.

(c) Prepaid insurance expired over past three months, $100.

(d) Depreciation on lawn care equipment for past three months, $260.

Problem 10-2B involves entering the June transactions for Claussen's Green Thumb in the general journal, processing adjusting entries, generating financial statements, and changing the accounting period.

Follow the step-by-step instructions below to complete the problem.

STEP 1:   **Start up the QuickBooks software.**

Choose QuickBooks Pro from the Start button.

STEP 2:   **Restore the Opening Balance data for Problem 10-2B.**

▶   **From the File menu, choose Restore.**

▶   **When the Restore From window appears, select "10-02B.QBB" and click on Open.**

▶   **When the Restore To window appears, use the Save in option to select the folder in which you wish to store your QuickBooks files, key a file name, and click on Save.**

The file name that you choose should identify the file as yours (10-02B Jane Doe). QuickBooks will add an extension of QBW.

▶   **If the file already exists, you will get a caution message. You must key "YES" and click OK to overwrite an existing file.**

STEP 3:   **From the Company menu, choose the Make Journal Entry option and key the transactions for June, 2002.**

Note: If the transaction involves accounts payable, you must enter or select from the drop list in the Name field, the vendor name.

STEP 4:   **Display the June Journal Report from the Memorized Reports list.**

STEP 5:   **Display the Trial Balance Report from the Memorized Reports list.**

STEP 6:   **Enter the adjusting entries for June 30, 2002 using the Make Journal Entry option. Key Adjusting Entry in the Memo field for each adjusting entry.**

STEP 7:   **Display the adjusting entries using the Adjusting Entries Journal Report option from the Memorized Reports list.**

STEP 8: Display the Income Statement Report from the Memorized Reports list.

STEP 9: Display the Balance Sheet Report from the Memorized Reports list.

STEP 10: Enter the closing entry to close the drawing account to capital on July 1, 2002.

STEP 11: Display the Post-Closing Trial Balance Report from the Memorized Reports list.

It isn't necessary to make closing entries to close out revenue and expense accounts. QuickBooks controls the process by date. Notice that the trial balance report as of July 1, 2002 (the beginning of a new fiscal period) has the revenue and expense accounts closed to Capital.

CHAPTER 10 MASTERY PROBLEM

John McRoe opened a tennis resort in June 2000. Most guests register for one week, arriving on Sunday afternoon and returning home the following Saturday afternoon. Guests stay at an adjacent hotel. The tennis resort provides lunch and dinner. Dining and exercise facilities are provided in a building rented by McRoe. A dietitian, masseuse, physical therapist, and athletic trainers are on call to assure the proper combination of diet and exercise. The chart of accounts and transactions for the month of June are provided below. McRoe uses the modified cash basis of accounting.

McRoe Tennis Resort

McRoe Tennis Resort
Chart of Accounts

Assets
101   Cash
142   Office Supplies
144   Food Supplies
184   Tennis Facilities
184.1 Accum. Depr.—Tennis Facilities
186   Exercise Equipment
186.1 Accum. Depr.—Exercise Equip.

Liabilities
202   Accounts Payable

Owner's Equity
311   John McRoe, Capital
312   John McRoe, Drawing
313   Income Summary

Revenues
401   Registration Fees

Expenses
511   Wages Expense
521   Rent Expense
523   Office Supplies Expense
524   Food Supplies Expense
525   Telephone Expense
533   Utilities Expense
535   Insurance Expense
536   Postage Expense
541   Depr. Exp.—Tennis Facilities
542   Depr. Exp.—Exercise Equip.

June 1   McRoe invested cash in the business, $90,000.

   1   Paid for new exercise equipment, $9,000.

   2   Deposited registration fees in the bank, $15,000.

   2   Paid rent for month of June on building and land, $2,500.

   2   Rogers Construction completed work on new tennis courts that cost $70,000. The estimated useful life of the facility is five years, at which time the courts will have to be resurfaced. Arrangements were made to pay the bill in July.

   3   Purchased food supplies on account from Au Naturel Foods, $5,000.

   5   Purchased office supplies on account from Gordon Office Supplies, $300.

   7   Deposited registration fees in the bank, $16,200.

10	Purchased food supplies on account from Au Naturel Foods, $6,200.
10	Paid wages to staff, $500.
14	Deposited registration fees in the bank, $13,500.
16	Purchased food supplies on account from Au Naturel Foods, $4,000.
17	Paid wages to staff, $500.
18	Paid postage, $85.
21	Deposited registration fees in the bank, $15,200.
24	Purchased food supplies on account from Au Naturel Foods, $5,500.
24	Paid wages to staff, $500.
28	Deposited registration fees in the bank, $14,000.
30	Purchased food supplies on account from Au Naturel Foods, $6,000.
30	Paid wages to staff, $500.
30	Paid Au Naturel Foods on account, $28,700.
30	Paid utility bill, $500.
30	Paid telephone bill, $120.
30	McRoe withdrew cash for personal use, $1,500.

The Chapter 10 Mastery Problem involves entering transactions in the general journal, displaying a journal report, and displaying a trial balance report. Follow the step-by-step instructions below to complete the problem.

STEP 1:   Start up the QuickBooks software.

Choose QuickBooks Pro from the Start button.

STEP 2:   Restore the Opening Balance data for the Chapter 10 Mastery Problem.

▶ **From the File menu, choose Restore.**

▶ **When the Restore From window appears, select "10 Mastery Problem.QBB" and click on Open.**

▶ **When the Restore To window appears, use the Save in option to select the folder in which you wish to store your QuickBooks files, key a file name, and click on Save.**

The file name that you choose should identify the file as yours (10 Mastery Jane Doe). QuickBooks will add an extension of QBW.

▶ **If the file already exists, you will get a caution message. You must key "YES" and click OK to overwrite an existing file.**

STEP 3:   From the Company menu, choose the Make Journal Entry option and key the transactions for June, 2002.

Note: If the transaction involves accounts payable, you must enter or select from the drop list in the Name field, the vendor name.

STEP 4:   From the Memorized Reports list, display the following reports:

June Journal Report

General Ledger Report

Trial Balance Report

CHAPTER 11 DEMONSTRATION PROBLEM

Karen Hunt operates Hunt's Audio-Video Store. The following transactions related to sales on account and cash receipts occurred during April 2000.

April 3   Sold merchandise on account to Susan Haberman, $159.50 plus tax of $11.17. Sale no. 41.

4   Sold merchandise on account to Goro Kimura, $299.95 plus tax of $21.00. Sale no. 42.

6   Received payment from Tera Scherrer on account, $69.50.

7   Issued a credit memo to Kenneth Watt for merchandise returned that had been sold on account, $42.75 including tax of $2.80.

10   Received payment from Kellie Cokley on account, $99.95.

11   Sold merchandise on account to Victor Cardona, $499.95 plus tax of $35.00. Sale no. 43.

14   Received payment from Kenneth Watt in full settlement of account, $157.00.

17   Sold merchandise on account to Susan Haberman, $379.95 plus tax of $26.60. Sale no. 44.

19   Sold merchandise on account to Tera Scherrer, $59.95 plus tax of $4.20. Sale no. 45.

21   Issued a credit memo to Goro Kimura for merchandise returned that had been sold on account, $53.45 including tax of $3.50.

24   Received payment from Victor Cardona on account, $299.95.

25   Sold merchandise on account to Kellie Cokley, $179.50 plus tax of $12.57. Sale no. 46.

26   Received payment from Susan Haberman on account, $250.65.

28   Sold merchandise on account to Kenneth Watt, $49.95 plus tax of $3.50. Sale no. 47.

30   Bank credit card sales for the month, $1,220.00 plus tax of $85.40. Bank credit card expense on these sales, $65.27.

30   Cash sales for the month, $2,000.00 plus tax of $140.00.

Hunt had the following general ledger account balances as of April 1:

Account Title	Account No.	General Ledger Balance on April 1
Cash	101	$5,000.00
Accounts Receivable	122	1,208.63
Sales Tax Payable	231	72.52
Sales	401	8,421.49
Sales Returns and Allowances	401.1	168.43
Bank Credit Card Expense	513	215.00

Hunt also had the following accounts receivable ledger account balances as of April 1:

Customer	Accounts Receivable Balance
Victor Cardona 6300 Washington Blvd. St. Louis, MO 63130-9523	$299.95
Kellie Cokley 4220 Kingsbury Blvd. St. Louis, MO 63130-1645	$99.95
Susan Haberman 9421 Garden Ct. Kirkwood, MO 63122-1878	$79.98
Goro Kimura 6612 Arundel Pl. Clayton, MO 63150-9266	$379.50

Tera Scherrer
315 W. Linden St.
Webster Groves, MO 63119-9881 $149.50

Kenneth Watt
11742 Fawnridge Dr.
St. Louis, MO 63131-1726 $199.75

Follow the steps below to complete the problem.

STEP 1:   **Start up the QuickBooks software.**

Choose QuickBooks Pro from the Start button.

STEP 2:   **Restore the Opening Balance data for the Chapter 11 Demonstration Problem.**

▶ **From the File menu, choose Restore.**

▶ **When the Restore From window appears, select "11 Demonstration Problem.QBB" and click on Open.**

▶ **When the Restore To window appears, use the Save in option to select the folder in which you wish to store your QuickBooks files, key a file name, and click on Save.**

The file name that you choose should identify the file as yours (11 Demo Jane Doe). QuickBooks will add an extension of QBW.

▶ **If the file already exists, you will get a caution message. You must key "YES" and click OK to overwrite an existing file.**

STEP 3:   **From the Company menu, choose the Make Journal Entry option and key the transactions for April, 2002. The first journal entry is illustrated in the General Journal Entry window shown in Figure 2.17.**

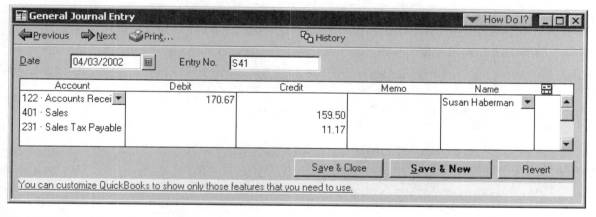

FIGURE 2.17 General Journal Entry Window

Note: If the transaction involves accounts receivable, you must enter or select from the drop list in the Name field, the customer name. Key the Sale No. in the Entry No. field.

STEP 4:   **From the Memorized Reports list, display the following reports:**

April Journal Report

General Ledger Report

Schedule of Accounts Receivable (Customer Balance Summary)

See the Solution section of this workbook for the solution to this demonstration problem.

PROBLEM 11-3A

Owens Distributors is a retail business. The following sales, returns, and cash receipts occurred during March 2000. There is an 8% sales tax. Beginning general ledger account balances were: Cash, $9,741.00; and Accounts Receivable, $1,058.25. Beginning customer account balances were: Thompson Group, $1,058.25.

March	1	Sale no. 33C to Able & Co., $1,800 plus sales tax.
	3	Sale no. 33D to R. J. Kalas, Inc., $2,240 plus sales tax.
	5	Able & Co. returned merchandise from sale no. 33C for a credit (credit memo no. 66), $30 plus sales tax.
	7	Cash sales for the week, $3,160 plus sales tax.
	10	Received payment from Able & Co. for sale no. 33C less credit memo no. 66.
	11	Sale no. 33E to Blevins Bakery, $1,210 plus sales tax.
	13	Received payment from R. J. Kalas for sale no. 33D.
	14	Cash sales for the week, $4,200 plus sales tax.
	16	Blevins Bakery returned merchandise from sale no. 33E for a credit (credit memo no. 67), $44 plus sales tax.
	18	Sale no. 33F to R. J. Kalas, Inc., $2,620 plus sales tax.
	20	Received payment from Blevins Bakery for sale no. 33E less credit memo no. 67.
	21	Cash sales for the week, $2,400 plus sales tax.
	25	Sale no. 33G to Blevins Bakery, $1,915 plus sales tax.
	27	Sale no. 33H to Thompson Group, $2,016 plus sales tax.
	28	Cash sales for the week, $3,500 plus sales tax.

Follow the steps listed to complete the problem.

STEP 1:   Start up the QuickBooks software.

Choose QuickBooks Pro from the Start button.

STEP 2:   Restore the Opening Balance data for Problem 11-3A.

▶ **From the File menu, choose Restore.**

▶ **When the Restore From window appears, select "Problem 11-03A.QBB" and click on Open.**

▶ **When the Restore To window appears, use the Save in option to select the folder in which you wish to store your QuickBooks files, key a file name, and click on Save.**

The file name that you choose should identify the file as yours (11-03A Jane Doe). QuickBooks will add an extension of QBW.

▶ **If the file already exists, you will get a caution message. You must key "YES" and click OK to overwrite an existing file.**

STEP 3:   From the Company menu, choose the Make Journal Entry option and key the transactions for March, 2002.

Note: If the transaction involves accounts receivable, you must enter or select from the drop list in the Name field, the customer name. Key the Sale No. in the Entry No. field.

STEP 4:   From the Memorized Reports list, display the following reports:

March Journal Report

General Ledger Report

Accounts Receivable Ledger (Customer Balance Detail)

Schedule of Accounts Receivable (Customer Balance Summary)

PROBLEM 11-3B

Paul Jackson owns a retail business. The following sales, returns, and cash receipts are for April 2000. There is a 7% sales tax.

April 1   Sale no. 111 to O. L. Meyers, $2,100 plus sales tax.

     3   Sale no. 112 to Andrew Plaa, $1,000 plus sales tax.

     6   O. L. Meyers returned merchandise from sale no. 111 for a credit (credit memo no. 42), $50 plus sales tax.

     7   Cash sales for the week, $3,240 plus sales tax.

     9   Received payment from O. L. Meyers for sale no. 111 less credit memo no. 42.

   12   Sale no. 113 to Melissa Richfield, $980 plus sales tax.

   14   Cash sales for the week, $2,180 plus sales tax.

   17   Melissa Richfield returned merchandise from sale no. 113 for a credit (credit memo no. 43), $40 plus sales tax.

   19   Sale no. 114 to Kelsay Munkres, $1,020 plus sales tax.

   21   Cash sales for the week, $2,600 plus sales tax.

   24   Sale no. 115 to O. L. Meyers, $920 plus sales tax.

   27   Sale no. 116 to Andrew Plaa, $1,320 plus sales tax.

   28   Cash sales for the week, $2,800 plus sales tax.

Beginning general ledger account balances:

Cash	$2,864.54
Accounts Receivable	2,726.25

Beginning customer account balances:

O. L. Meyers	$2,186.00
K. Munkres	482.00
M. Richfield	58.25

Follow the steps listed to complete the problem.

STEP 1:   **Start up the QuickBooks software.**

Choose QuickBooks Pro from the Start button.

STEP 2:   **Restore the Opening Balance data for Problem 11-3B.**

▶ **From the File menu, choose Restore.**

▶ **When the Restore From window appears, select "Problem 11-03B.QBB" and click on Open.**

▶ **When the Restore To window appears, use the Save in option to select the folder in which you wish to store your QuickBooks files, key a file name, and click on Save.**

The file name that you choose should identify the file as yours (11-03B Jane Doe). QuickBooks will add an extension of QBW.

▶ **If the file already exists, you will get a caution message. You must key "YES" and click OK to overwrite an existing file.**

STEP 3:   **From the Company menu, choose the Make Journal Entry option and key the transactions for April, 2002.**

Note: If the transaction involves accounts receivable, you must enter or select from the drop list in the Name field, the customer name. Key the Sale No. in the Entry No. field.

STEP 4:   **From the Memorized Reports list, display the following reports:**

April Journal Report

General Ledger Report

Accounts Receivable Ledger (Customer Balance Detail)

Schedule of Accounts Receivable (Customer Balance Summary)

CHAPTER 11 MASTERY PROBLEM

Geoff and Sandy Harland own and operate Wayward Kennel and Pet Supply. Their motto is, "If your pet is not becoming to you, he should be coming to us." The Harlands maintain a sales tax payable account throughout the month to account for the 6% sales tax. They use a sales journal, a cash receipts journal, and a general journal. The following sales and cash collections took place during the month of September.

Sept. 2   Sold a fish aquarium on account to Ken Shank, $125.00 plus tax of $7.50, terms n/30. Sale no. 101.

    3   Sold dog food on account to Nancy Truelove, $68.25 plus tax of $4.10, terms n/30. Sale no. 102.

    5   Sold a bird cage on account to Jean Warkentin, $43.95 plus tax of $2.64, terms n/30. Sale no. 103.

    8   Cash sales for the week, $2,332.45 plus tax of $139.95.

  10   Received cash for boarding and grooming services, $625.00 plus tax of $37.50.

  11   Jean Warkentin stopped by the store to point out a minor defect in the bird cage purchased in sale no. 103. The Harlands offered a sales allowance of $10.00 plus tax on the price of the cage, which satisfied Warkentin.

  12   Sold a cockatoo on account to Tully Shaw, $1,200.00 plus tax of $72.00, terms n/30. Sale no. 104.

  14   Received cash on account from Rosa Alanso, $256.00.

  15   Rosa Alanso returned merchandise, $93.28 including tax of $5.28.

  15   Cash sales for the week, $2,656.85 plus tax of $159.41.

  16   Received cash on account from Nancy Truelove, $58.25.

  18   Received cash for boarding and grooming services, $535.00 plus tax of $32.10.

  19   Received cash on account from Ed Cochran, $63.25.

  20   Sold pet supplies on account to Susan Hays, $83.33 plus tax of $5.00, terms n/30. Sale no. 105.

  21   Sold three Labrador Retriever puppies to All American Day Camp, $375.00 plus tax of $22.50, terms n/30. Sale no. 106.

  22   Cash sales for the week, $3,122.45 plus tax of $187.35.

  23   Received cash for boarding and grooming services, $515.00 plus tax of $30.90.

  25   Received cash on account from Ken Shank, $132.50.

  26   Received cash on account from Nancy Truelove, $72.35.

  27   Received cash on account from Joe Gloy, $273.25.

  28   Borrowed cash to purchase a pet limousine, $11,000.00.

  29   Cash sales for the week, $2,835.45 plus tax of $170.13.

  30   Received cash for boarding and grooming services, $488.00 plus tax of $29.28.

Wayward had the following general ledger account balances as of September 1:

Account Title	Account No.	General Ledger Balance on Sept. 1
Cash	101	$23,500.25
Accounts Receivable	122	850.75
Notes Payable	201	2,500.00
Sales Tax Payable	231	909.90
Sales	401	13,050.48
Sales Returns and Allowances	401.1	86.00
Boarding and Grooming Revenue	402	2,115.00

Wayward also had the following accounts receivable ledger balances as of September 1:

Customer	Accounts Receivable Balance
Rosa Alanso 2541 East 2nd Street Bloomington, IN 47401-5356	$456.00
Ed Cochran 2669 Windcrest Drive Bloomington, IN 47401-5446	$63.25
Joe Gloy 1458 Parnell Avenue Muncie, IN 47304-2682	$273.25
Nancy Truelove 2300 E. National Road Cumberland, IN 46229-4824	$58.25

New customers opening accounts during September were:

All American Day Camp
3025 Old Mill Run
Bloomington, IN 47408-1080

Tully Shaw
3315 Longview Avenue
Bloomington, IN 47401-7223

Susan Hays
1424 Jackson Creek Road
Nashville, IN 47448-2245

Jean Warkentin
1813 Deep Well Court
Bloomington, IN 47401-5124

Ken Shank
6422 E. Bender Road
Bloomington, IN 47401-7756

Follow the steps listed to complete the problem.

STEP 1: **Start up the QuickBooks software.**

Choose QuickBooks Pro from the Start button.

STEP 2: **Restore the Opening Balance data for the Chapter 11 Mastery Problem.**

▶ **From the File menu, choose Restore.**

▶ **When the Restore From window appears, select "11 Mastery Problem.QBB" and click on Open.**

▶ **When the Restore To window appears, use the Save in option to select the folder in which you wish to store your QuickBooks files, key a file name, and click on Save.**

The file name that you choose should identify the file as yours (11 Mastery Jane Doe). QuickBooks will add an extension of QBW.

▶ **If the file already exists, you will get a caution message. You must key "YES" and click OK to overwrite an existing file.**

STEP 3: **From the Company menu, choose the Make Journal Entry option and key the transactions for September, 2002.**

Note: If the transaction involves accounts receivable, you must enter or select from the drop list in the Name field, the customer name. Key the Sale No. in the Entry No. field.

STEP 4: **From the Memorized Reports list, display the following reports:**

September Journal Report

General Ledger Report

Schedule of Accounts Receivable (Customer Balance Summary)

Accounts Receivable Ledger (Customer Balance Detail)

CHAPTER 12 DEMONSTRATION PROBLEM

Jodi Rutman operates a retail pharmacy called Rutman Pharmacy. The following are the transactions related to purchases and cash payments for the month of June 2000.

June 1   Purchased merchandise from Sullivan Co. on account, $234.20. Invoice no. 71 dated June 1, terms 2/10, n/30.

2   Issued check no. 536 for payment of June rent (Rent Expense), $1,000.00.

5   Purchased merchandise from Amfac Drug Supply on account, $562.40. Invoice no. 196 dated June 2, terms 1/15, n/30.

7   Purchased merchandise from University Drug Co. on account, $367.35. Invoice no. 914A dated June 5, terms 3/10 eom, n/30.

9   Issued check no. 537 to Sullivan Co. in payment of invoice no. 71 less 2% discount.

12   Received a credit memo from Amfac Drug Supply for merchandise returned that was purchased on June 5, $46.20.

14   Purchased merchandise from Mutual Drug Co. on account, $479.40. Invoice no. 745 dated June 14, terms 2/10, n/30.

15   Received a credit memo from University Drug Co. for merchandise returned that was purchased on June 7, $53.70.

16   Issued check no. 538 to Amfac Drug Supply in payment of invoice no. 196 less the credit memo of June 12 and less 1% discount.

23   Issued check no. 539 to Mutual Drug Co. in payment of invoice no. 745 less 2% discount.

27   Purchased merchandise from Flites Pharmaceuticals on account, $638.47. Invoice no. 675 dated June 27, terms 2/10 eom, n/30.

29   Issued check no. 540 to Dolgin Candy Co. for a cash purchase of merchandise, $270.20.

30   Issued check no. 541 to Vashon Medical Supply in payment of invoice no. 416, $1,217.69. No discount allowed.

Follow the steps listed to complete the Chapter 12 Demonstration Problem.

STEP 1:   **Start up the QuickBooks software.**

Choose QuickBooks Pro from the Start button.

STEP 2:   **Restore the Opening Balance data for the Chapter 12 Demonstration Problem.**

▶   **From the File menu, choose Restore.**

▶   **When the Restore From window appears, select "12 Demonstration Problem.QBB" and click on Open.**

▶   **When the Restore To window appears, use the Save in option to select the folder in which you wish to store your QuickBooks files, key a file name, and click on Save.**

The file name that you choose should identify the file as yours (12 Demo Jane Doe). QuickBooks will add an extension of QBW.

▶   **If the file already exists, you will get a caution message. You must key "YES" and click OK to overwrite an existing file.**

STEP 3:   From the Company menu, choose the Make Journal Entry option and key the transactions for June, 2002. The first transaction is illustrated in the General Journal Entry window shown in Figure 2.18.

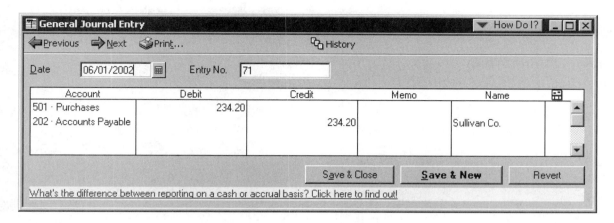

FIGURE 2.18 General Journal Entry Window

> Note: If the transaction involves accounts payable, you must enter or select from the drop list in the Name field, the vendor name. Key the Invoice No. and Check No. in the Entry No. field.

STEP 4:   From the Memorized Reports list, display the following reports:

June Journal Report

General Ledger Report

Schedule of Accounts Payable (Vendor Balance Summary)

Accounts Payable Ledger (Vendor Balance Detail)

See the Solution section of this workbook for the solution to this demonstration problem.

PROBLEM 12-3A

Freddy Flint owns a small retail business called Flint's Fantasy. The cash account has a balance of $20,000 on July 1. The following transactions occurred during July.

July 1   Issued check no. 414 in payment of July rent, $1,500.
  1   Purchased merchandise on account from Tang's Toys, invoice no. 311, $2,700, terms 2/10, n/30.
  3   Purchased merchandise on account from Sillas & Company, invoice no. 812, $3,100, terms 1/10, n/30.
  5   Returned merchandise purchased from Tang's Toys, receiving a credit memo on the amount owed, $500.
  8   Purchased merchandise on account from Daisy's Dolls, invoice no. 139, $1,900, terms 2/10, n/30.
  11   Issued check no. 415 to Tang's Toys for merchandise purchased on account, less return of July 5 and less 2% discount.
  13   Issued a check no. 416 to Sillas & Company for merchandise purchased on account, less 1% discount.
  15   Returned merchandise purchased from Daisy's Dolls, receiving a credit memo on the amount owed, $400.
  18   Issued check no. 417 to Daisy's Dolls for merchandise purchased on account, less return of July 15 and less 2% discount.

25   Purchased merchandise on account from Allied Business, invoice no. 489, $2,450, terms n/30.
26   Purchased merchandise on account from Tang's Toys, invoice no. 375, $1,980, terms 2/10, n/30.
29   Purchased merchandise on account from Sillas & Company, invoice no. 883, $3,460, terms 1/10, n/30.
31   Freddy Flint withdrew cash for personal use, $2,000. Issued check no. 418.
31   Issued check no. 419 to Glisan Distributors for a cash purchase of merchandise, $975.

Follow the steps listed to complete the problem.

STEP 1:   **Start up the QuickBooks software.**

Choose QuickBooks Pro from the Start button.

STEP 2:   **Restore the Opening Balance data for Problem 12-3A.**

▶   **From the File menu, choose Restore.**

▶   **When the Restore From window appears, select "Problem 12-03A.QBB" and click on Open.**

▶   **When the Restore To window appears, use the Save in option to select the folder in which you wish to store your QuickBooks files, key a file name, and click on Save.**

The file name that you choose should identify the file as yours (12-03A Jane Doe). QuickBooks will add an extension of QBW.

▶   **If the file already exists, you will get a caution message. You must key "YES" and click OK to overwrite an existing file.**

STEP 3:   **From the Company menu, choose the Make Journal Entry option and key the transactions for July, 2002.**

Note: If the transaction involves accounts payable, you must enter or select from the drop list in the Name field, the vendor name. Key the Invoice No. and Check No. in the Entry No. field.

STEP 4:   **From the Memorized Reports list, display the following reports:**

July Journal Report

General Ledger Report

Schedule of Accounts Payable (Vendor Balance Summary)

Accounts Payable Ledger (Vendor Balance Detail)

PROBLEM 12-3B

Debbie Mueller owns a small retail business called Debbie's Doll House. The cash account has a balance of $20,000 on July 1. The following transactions occurred during July.

July 1   Issued check no. 314 for July rent, $1,400.
    1   Purchased merchandise on account from Topper's Toys, invoice no. 211, $2,500, terms 2/10, n/30.
    3   Purchased merchandise on account from Jones & Company, invoice no. 812, $2,800, terms 1/10, n/30.
    5   Returned merchandise purchased from Topper's Toys receiving a credit memo on the amount owed, $400.
    8   Purchased merchandise on account from Downtown Merchants, invoice no. 159, $1,600, terms 2/10, n/30.
    11   Issued check no. 315 to Topper's Toys for merchandise purchased on account, less return of July 5 and less 2% discount.

13   Issued check no. 316 to Jones & Company for merchandise purchased on account, less 1% discount.

15   Returned merchandise purchased from Downtown Merchants receiving a credit memo on the amount owed, $600.

18   Issued check no. 317 to Downtown Merchants for merchandise purchased on account, less return of July 15 and less 2% discount.

25   Purchased merchandise on account from Columbia Products, invoice no. 468, $3,200, terms n/30.

26   Purchased merchandise on account from Topper's Toys, invoice no. 395, $1,430, terms 2/10, n/30.

29   Purchased merchandise on account from Jones & Company, invoice no. 853, $2,970, terms 1/10, n/30.

31   Mueller withdrew cash for personal use, $2,500. Issued check no. 318.

31   Issued check no. 319 to Burnside Warehouse for a cash purchase of merchandise, $1,050.

Follow the steps listed to complete the problem.

STEP 1:   **Start up the QuickBooks software.**

Choose QuickBooks Pro from the Start button.

STEP 2:   **Restore the Opening Balance data for Problem 12-3B.**

▶   **From the File menu, choose Restore.**

▶   **When the Restore From window appears, select "Problem 12-03B.QBB" and click on Open.**

▶   **When the Restore To window appears, use the Save in option to select the folder in which you wish to store your QuickBooks files, key a file name, and click on Save.**

The file name that you choose should identify the file as yours (12-03B Jane Doe). QuickBooks will add an extension of QBW.

▶   **If the file already exists, you will get a caution message. You must key "YES" and click OK to overwrite an existing file.**

STEP 3:   **From the Company menu, choose the Make Journal Entry option and key the transactions for July, 2002.**

Note: If the transaction involves accounts payable, you must enter or select from the drop list in the Name field, the vendor name. Key the Invoice No. and Check No. in the Entry No. field.

STEP 4:   **From the Memorized Reports list, display the following reports:**

July Journal Report

General Ledger Report

Schedule of Accounts Payable (Vendor Balance Summary)

Accounts Payable Ledger (Vendor Balance Detail)

CHAPTER 12 MASTERY PROBLEM

Michelle French owns and operates Books and More, a retail book store. Selected account balances on June 1 are as follows:

General Ledger

Cash	$32,200.00
Accounts Payable	2,000.00
Michelle French, Drawing	18,000.00
Purchases	67,021.66

Purchases Returns and Allowances	2,315.23		
Purchases Discounts	905.00		
Freight-In	522.60		
Rent Expense	3,125.00		
Utilities Expense	1,522.87		

Accounts Payable Ledger

North-Eastern Publishing Co. $2,000.00

The following purchases and cash payment transactions took place during the month of June:

June 1   Purchased books on account from Irving Publishing Co., $2,100. Invoice no. 101, terms 2/10, n/30, FOB destination.

     2   Issued check no. 300 to North-Eastern Publishing Co. for goods purchased on May 23, terms 2/10, n/30, $1,960 (the $2,000 invoice amount less the 2% discount).

     3   Purchased books on account from Broadway Publishing, Inc., $2,880. Invoice no. 711, subject to 20% trade discount, and invoice terms of 3/10, n/30, FOB shipping point.

     3   Issued check no. 301 to Mayday Shipping for delivery from Broadway Publishing, Inc., $250.

     4   Issued check no. 302 for June rent, $625.

     8   Purchased books on account from North-Eastern Publishing Co., $5,825. Invoice no. 268, terms 2/eom, n/60, FOB destination.

   10   Received a credit memo from Irving Publishing Co., $550. Books had been returned because the covers were on upside down.

   13   Issued check no. 304 to Broadway Publishing, Inc., for the purchase made on June 3. (Check no. 303 was voided because an error was made in preparing it.)

   28   Made the following purchases:

Invoice No.	Company	Amount	Terms
579	Broadway Publishing, Inc.	$2,350	2/10, n/30 FOB destination
406	North-Eastern Publishing Co.	4,200	2/eom, n/60 FOB destination
964	Riley Publishing Co.	3,450	3/10, n/30 FOB destination

   30   Issued check no. 305 to Taylor County Utility Co., for June utilities, $325.

   30   French withdrew cash for personal use, $4,500. Issued check no. 306.

   30   Issued check no. 307 to Irving Publishing Co. for purchase made on June 1 less returns made on June 10.

   30   Issued check no. 308 to North-Eastern Publishing Co. for purchase made on June 8.

   30   Issued check no. 309 for books purchased at an auction, $1,328.

Follow the steps listed to complete the problem.

STEP 1:   Start up the QuickBooks software.

Choose QuickBooks Pro from the Start button.

STEP 2:   Restore the Opening Balance data for the Chapter 12 Mastery Problem.

▶   **From the File menu, choose Restore.**

▶   **When the Restore From window appears, select "12 Mastery Problem.QBB" and click on Open.**

▶   **When the Restore To window appears, use the Save in option to select the folder in which you wish to store your QuickBooks files, key a file name, and click on Save.**

The file name that you choose should identify the file as yours (12 Mastery Jane Doe). QuickBooks will add an extension of QBW.

► If the file already exists, you will get a caution message. You must key "YES" and click OK to overwrite an existing file.

STEP 3: From the Company menu, choose the Make Journal Entry option and key the transactions for June, 2002.

Note: If the transaction involves accounts payable, you must enter or select from the drop list in the Name field, the vendor name. Key the Invoice No. and Check No. in the Entry No. field.

STEP 4: From the Memorized Reports list, display the following reports:

June Journal Report

General Ledger Report

Schedule of Accounts Payable (Vendor Balance Summary)

Accounts Payable Ledger (Vendor Balance Detail)

CHAPTER 13 DEMONSTRATION PROBLEM

During the month of May, 2000, David's Specialty Shop engaged in the following transactions:

May 1   Sold merchandise on account to Molly Mac, $2,000 plus tax of $100. Sale no. 533.

2   Issued check no. 750 to Kari Co. in partial payment of May 1 balance, $800 less 2% discount.

3   Purchased merchandise on account from Scanlan Wholesalers $2,000. Invoice no. 621, dated May 3, terms 2/10, n/30.

4   Purchased merchandise on account from Simpson Enterprises $1,500. Invoice no. 767, dated May 4, 2/15, n/30.

4   Issued check no. 751 in payment of telephone expense for the month of December, $200.

8   Sold merchandise for cash, $3,600, plus tax of $180.

9   Received payment from Cody Slaton in full settlement of Invoice no 480, $2,500.

10   Issued check no. 752 to Scanlan Wholesalers in payment of May 1 balance of $1200.

12   Sold merchandise on account to Cody Slaton, $3,000 plus tax of $150. Sale no. 534.

12   Received payment from Kori Reynolds on account, $2,100.

13   Issued check no. 753 to Simpson Enterprises in payment of May 4 purchase. Invoice no. 767, less 2% discount.

13   Cody Slayton returned merchandise for credit, $1,000 plus sales tax, $50.00. Invoice no. 480.

17   Returned merchandise to Johnson Essentials for credit towards Invoice no. 580, $500.

22   Received payment from Natalie Gabbert on account, $1,555.

27   Sold merchandise on account to Natalie Gabbert, $2,000 plus tax of $100. Sale no. 535.

29   Issued check no. 754 in payment of wages (Wages Expense) for the four-week period ending May 30, $1,100.

Follow the steps listed to complete the problem.

STEP 1: Start up the QuickBooks software.

Choose QuickBooks Pro from the Start button.

STEP 2: Restore the Opening Balance data for the Chapter 13 Demonstration Problem.

► From the File menu, choose Restore.

► When the Restore From window appears, select "13 Demonstration Problem.QBB" and click on Open.

► When the Restore To window appears, use the Save in option to select the folder in which you wish to store your QuickBooks files, key a file name, and click on Save.

The file name that you choose should identify the file as yours (13 Demo Jane Doe). QuickBooks will add an extension of QBW.

▶ **If the file already exists, you will get a caution message. You must key "YES" and click OK to overwrite an existing file.**

STEP 3:   From the Company menu, choose the Make Journal Entry option and key the transactions for May, 2002. The first journal, affecting accounts receivable, in the General Journal Entry window is shown in Figure 2.19. The next journal entry, affecting accounts payable, is shown in Figure 2.20.

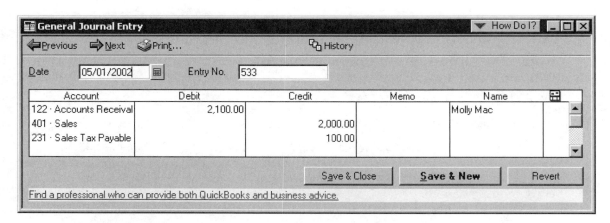

FIGURE 2.19 Accounts Receivable Entry in the General Journal Entry Window

FIGURE 2.20 Accounts Payable Entry in the General Journal Entry Window

Note: If the transaction involves accounts receivable, you must enter or select from the drop list in the Name field, the customer name. If the transaction involves accounts payable, you must enter or select from the drop list in the Name field, the vendor name. Key the Check No., Invoice No., or Sale No. in the Number field. Leave the Entry No. and Memo fields blank.

STEP 4:   From the Memorized Reports list, display the following reports:

General Journal Report

Trial Balance Report

General Ledger Report

Schedule of Accounts Receivable (Customer Balance Summary)

Schedule of Accounts Payable (Vendor Balance Summary)

See the Solution section of this workbook for the solution to this demonstration problem.

PROBLEM 13-2A

Zebra Imaginarium, a retail business, had the following cash receipts during December 2000. The sales tax is 6%.

Dec. 1   Received payment on account from Michael Anderson, $1,360.

2   Received payment on account from Ansel Manufacturing, $382.

7   Cash sales for the week, $3,160 plus tax. Bank credit card sales for the week, $1,000 plus tax. Bank credit card fee is 3%.

8   Received payment on account from J. Gorbea, $880.

11   Michael Anderson returned merchandise for a credit, $60 plus tax.; Invoice no. 892.

14   Cash sales for the week, $2,800 plus tax. Bank credit card sales for the week, $800 plus tax. Bank credit card fee is 3%.

20   Received payment on account from Tom Wilson, $1,110.

21   Ansel Manufacturing returned merchandise for a credit,. $22 plus tax; Invoice no. 902

21   Cash sales for the week, $3,200 plus tax.

24   Received payment on account from Rachel Carson, $2,000.

Follow the steps listed to complete the problem.

STEP 1:   **Start up the QuickBooks software.**

Choose QuickBooks Pro from the Start button.

STEP 2:   **Restore the Opening Balance data for Problem 13-2A.**

▶   **From the File menu, choose Restore.**

▶   **When the Restore From window appears, select "13-02A.QBB" and click on Open.**

▶   **When the Restore To window appears, use the Save in option to select the folder in which you wish to store your QuickBooks files, key a file name, and click on Save.**

The file name that you choose should identify the file as yours (13-02A Jane Doe) QuickBooks will add an extension of QBW.

▶   **If the file already exists, you will get a caution message. You must key "YES" and click OK to overwrite an existing file.**

STEP 3:   **From the Company menu, choose the Make Journal Entry option and key the transactions for December, 2002.**

Note: If the transaction involves accounts receivable, you must enter or select from the drop list in the Name field, the customer name. Leave the Entry No. and Memo fields blank.

STEP 4:   **From the Memorized Reports list, display the following reports:**

General Journal Report

Trial Balance Report

General Ledger Report

Schedule of Accounts Receivable (Customer Balance Summary)

PROBLEM 13-2B

Color Florists, a retail business, had the following cash receipts during January 2000. The sales tax is 5%.

Jan. 1   Received payment on account from Ray Boyd, $880.

    3   Received payment on account from Clint Hassell, $271.

    5   Cash sales for the week, $2,800 plus tax. Bank credit card sales for the week, $1,200 plus tax. Bank credit card fee is 3%.

    8   Received payment on account from Jan Sowada, $912.

  11   Ray Boyd returned merchandise for a credit, $40 plus tax.; Invoice no. 892.

  12   Cash sales for the week, $3,100 plus tax. Bank credit card sales for the week, $1,900 plus tax. Bank credit card fee is 3%.

  15   Received payment on account from Robert Zehnle, $1,100.

  18   Robert Zehnle returned merchandise for a credit,. $31 plus tax; Invoice no. 902

  19   Cash sales for the week, $2,230 plus tax.

  25   Received payment on account from Dazai Manufacturing, $318.

Follow the steps listed to complete the problem.

STEP 1:   **Start up the QuickBooks software.**

Choose QuickBooks Pro from the Start button.

STEP 2:   **Restore the Opening Balance data for Problem 13-2B.**

▶ **From the File menu, choose Restore.**

▶ **When the Restore From window appears, select "13-02B.QBB" and click on Open.**

▶ **When the Restore To window appears, use the Save in option to select the folder in which you wish to store your QuickBooks files, key a file name, and click on Save.**

The file name that you choose should identify the file as yours (13-02B Jane Doe). QuickBooks will add an extension of QBW.

▶ **If the file already exists, you will get a caution message. You must key "YES" and click OK to overwrite an existing file.**

STEP 3:   **From the Company menu, choose the Make Journal Entry option and key the transactions for January, 2002.**

Note: If the transaction involves accounts receivable, you must enter or select from the drop list in the Name field, the customer name. Leave the Entry No. and Memo fields blank.

STEP 4:   **From the Memorized Reports list, display the following reports:**

General Journal Report

Trial Balance Report

General Ledger Report

Schedule of Accounts Receivable (Customer Balance Summary)

CHAPTER 13 MASTERY PROBLEM

During the month of Oct, 2000, The Pink Petal flower shop engaged in the following transactions:

Oct 1   Sold merchandise on account to Elizabeth Shoemaker, $1,000 plus sales tax. Sale no. 222.

   2   Issued check no. 190 to Jill Hand in payment of October 1 balance of $500, less 2% discount.

2   Purchased merchandise on account from Flower Wholesalers $4,000. Invoice no. 500, dated October 2, terms 2/10, n/30.

4   Purchased merchandise on account from Seidl Enterprises $700. Invoice no. 527, dated October 4, terms 2/15, n/30.

5   Issued check no. 191 in payment of telephone expense for the month of September, $150.

7   Sold merchandise for cash, $3500, plus tax of $175.

9   Received payment from Leigh Summers in full settlement of account, $2,000.

11   Issued check no. 192 to Flower Wholesalers in payment of October 1 balance of $1,500.

12   Sold merchandise on account to Leigh Summers, $2,000 plus sales tax. Sale no. 223.

12   Received payment from Meg Johnson on account, $3,100.

13   Issued check no. 193 to Seidl Enterprises in payment of October 4 purchase.

14   Meg Johnson returned merchandise for a credit, $300 plus sales tax; Invoice no. 212.

17   Returned merchandise to Vases Etc. for credit, $900; Invoice no. 580.

24   Received payment from David's Decorating on account, $2,135.

27   Sold merchandise on account to David's Decorating, $3,000 plus sales tax. Sale no. 224.

29   Issured check no. 194 in payment of wages (Wages Expense) for the four-week period ending October 30, $900.

Follow the steps listed to complete the problem.

STEP 1:   **Start up the QuickBooks software.**

Choose QuickBooks Pro from the Start button.

STEP 2:   **Restore the Opening Balance data for the Chapter 13 Mastery Problem.**

▶   **From the File menu, choose Restore.**

▶   **When the Restore From window appears, select "13 Mastery Problem.QBB" and click on Open.**

▶   **When the Restore To window appears, use the Save in option to select the folder in which you wish to store your QuickBooks files, key a file name, and click on Save.**

The file name that you choose should identify the file as yours (13 Mastery Jane Doe). QuickBooks will add an extension of QBW.

▶   **If the file already exists, you will get a caution message. You must key "YES" and click OK to overwrite an existing file.**

STEP 3:   **From the Company menu, choose the Make Journal Entry option and key the transactions for October, 2002.**

Note: If the transaction involves accounts receivable, you must enter or select from the drop list in the Name field, the customer name. If the transaction involves accounts payable, you must enter or select from the drop list in the Name field, the vendor name. Enter the Check Number, Invoice Number, or Sale Number in the Entry No. field. Leave the Memo field blank.

STEP 4:   **From the Memorized Reports list, display the following reports:**

General Journal Report

Trial Balance Report

General Ledger Report

Schedule of Accounts Receivable (Customer Balance Summary)

Schedule of Accounts Payable (Vendor Balance Summary)

CHAPTER 14 DEMONSTRATION PROBLEM

Harpo, Inc., is a retail novelty store. The following transactions relate to operations for the month of March.

March 2   Issued voucher no. 313 to Tremont Rental for March rent, $500.

2   Issued check no. 450 to Tremont Rental, $500. Voucher no. 313.

3   Purchased merchandise from Gail's Gags, $550, terms 2/15, n/60. Voucher no. 314.

4   Purchased merchandise from Silly Sam's, $200, terms 2/10, n/60. Voucher no. 315.

10   Issued check no. 451 to Jerry's Jokes, $500 less $10 discount. Voucher no. 310.

12   Received a credit memo from Silly Sam's for returned merchandise that was purchased on March 4, $100.

14   Issued check no. 452 to Resource Supplies, $250. Voucher no. 311.

16   Purchased merchandise from Giggles, $700, terms 2/10, n/30. Voucher no. 316.

18   Issued check no. 453 to Gail's Gags for purchase made on March 3 less 2% discount. Voucher no. 314.

19   Issued check no. 454 to Donnelly's, $750. Voucher no. 312.

21   Purchased merchandise from Creations, $870, terms 3/15, n/50. Voucher no. 317.

25   Purchased supplies from Hal's Supply, $120, terms 3/10, n/30. Voucher no. 318.

31   Issued check no. 455 to Silly Sam's for purchase made on March 4 less returns made on March 12. Voucher no. 315.

31   Issued voucher no. 319 to Payroll in payment of March wages, $1,250.

31   Issued check no. 456 to Payroll, $1,250. Voucher no. 319.

Follow the step-by-step instructions provided to solve the problem.

STEP 1:   **Start up the QuickBooks software.**

Choose QuickBooks Pro from the Start button.

STEP 2:   **Restore the Opening Balance data for the Chapter 14 Demonstration Problem.**

▶   **From the File menu, choose Restore.**

▶   **When the Restore From window appears, select "14 Demonstration Problem.QBB" and click on Open.**

▶   **When the Restore To window appears, use the Save in option to select the folder in which you wish to store your QuickBooks files, key a file name, and click on Save.**

The file name that you choose should identify the file as yours (14 Demo Jane Doe). QuickBooks will add an extension of QBW.

▶   **If the file already exists, you will get a caution message. You must key "YES" and click OK to overwrite an existing file.**

STEP 3:   **Key the Voucher transactions for March, 2002 into the Vouchers Payable Register. From the Banking menu choose the Use Register option. When the Select Account window appears, choose Vouchers Payable. The Voucher Payable Register is shown in Figure 2.21.**

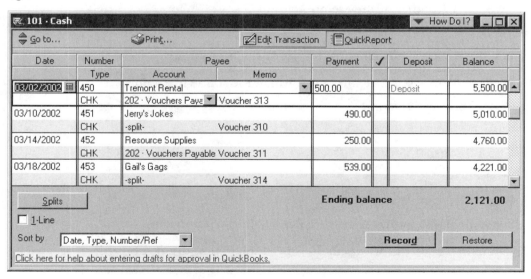

FIGURE 2.21 Vouchers Payable Register Window

▶ Key the date of the new voucher transaction.

▶ Key the Voucher Number into the Number field.

▶ Key or select the Vendor.

▶ Calculate and enter the Due Date.

▶ Key the Voucher amount in the Billed column.

▶ Key the account to be debited into the Account field.

▶ The computer will make the offsetting entry to Vouchers Payable.

▶ Record the transaction.

STEP 4: Key the cash payment transactions for March, 2002 into the Cash Register. From the Banking menu choose the Use Register option. When the Select Account window appears, choose Cash. Cash payment tgransactions in the Cash Register window are illustrated in Figure 2.22.

FIGURE 2.22 Cash Register Window

- ▶ Key the date of the new voucher transaction.
- ▶ Key the Check Number.
- ▶ Key or select the Vendor.
- ▶ Key the amount of the check in the Payment column.
- ▶ Key or select Vouchers Payable in the Account field. If a discount is involved, click on the Splits button. The split option allows you to enter a multi-part transaction. Key the discount amount as a negative number. The computer will make the offsetting entry to Cash. A split transaction in the Cash Register window is shown in Figure 2.23.

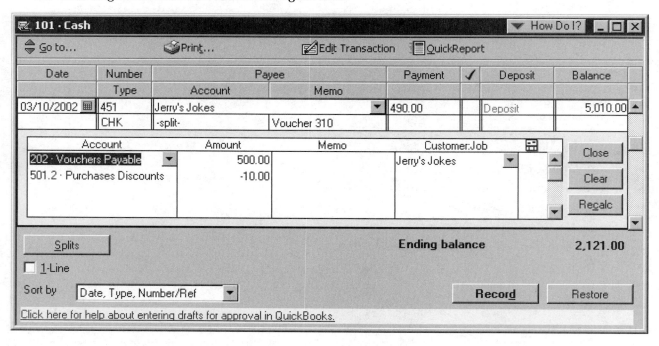

FIGURE 2.23 Split Transaction in the Cash Register Window

- ▶ Key the Voucher Number in the Memo field.
- ▶ Record the transaction.

STEP 5: Key the General Journal entry to record the merchandise return for March 12, 2002.

STEP 6: From the Memorized Reports list, display the following reports:

Vouchers Journal Report

Cash Payments Journal Report

General Journal Report

Trial Balance Report

General Ledger Report

Schedule of Accounts Payable (Vendor Balance Summary)

See the Solution section of this workbook for the solution to this demonstration problem.

PROBLEM 14-3A

Betty Classic owns the Classic Candle Shop. The following transactions occurred during April 2000. The Classic Candle Shop uses a voucher register, a check register, and a general ledger. Unpaid vouchers are filed and listed at the end of the month. General ledger account balances on April 1 were: Cash, $5,189; and Supplies, $408.

Date	Voucher No.	Issued To	Amount	Purpose	Terms
4/1	1101	Landmark Realty	$ 500	April rent	
4/3	1102	Wax House	280	Merchandise	2/10, n/30
4/5	1103	Designs West	490	Merchandise	2/10, n/30
4/9	1104	Crane Stationers	180	Office supplies	
4/11	1105	Magic Solutions	600	Merchandise	2/10, n/30
4/15	1106	Payroll	1,500	Bimonthly payroll	
4/23	1107	Wax House	510	Merchandise	1/10, n/30
4/25	1108	Baskets & More	440	Merchandise	2/10, n/30
4/28	1109	Magic Solutions	450	Merchandise	2/10, n/30
4/30	1110	Payroll	1,500	Bimonthly payroll	

Checks issued:

Date	Check No.	Payee	Voucher No.	Amount
4/1	928	Landmark Realty	1101	$ 500
4/9	929	Crane Stationers	1104	180
4/11	930	Wax House	1102	280
4/15	931	Payroll	1106	1,500
4/19	932	Designs West	1103	490
4/30	933	Payroll	1110	1,500

Follow the step-by-step instructions provided to solve the problem.

STEP 1:   **Start up the QuickBooks software.**

Choose QuickBooks Pro from the Start button.

STEP 2:   **Restore the Opening Balance data for Problem 14-3A.**

▶   **From the File menu, choose Restore.**

▶   **When the Restore From window appears, select "14-03A.QBB" and click on Open.**

▶   **When the Restore To window appears, use the Save in option to select the folder in which you wish to store your QuickBooks files, key a file name, and click on Save.**

The file name that you choose should identify the file as yours (14-03B Jane Doe). QuickBooks will add an extension of QBW.

▶   **If the file already exists, you will get a caution message. You must key "YES" and click OK to overwrite an existing file.**

STEP 3:   **Key the Voucher transactions for April, 2002 into the Vouchers Payable Register. From the Banking menu choose the Use Register option. When the Select Account window appears, choose Vouchers Payable.**

▶   **Key the date of the new voucher transaction.**

▶   **Key the Voucher Number into the Number field.**

▶   **Key or select the Vendor.**

- ▶ Calculate and enter the Due Date.

- ▶ Key the Voucher amount in the Billed column.

- ▶ Key the account to be debited into the Account field.

- ▶ The computer will make the offsetting entry to Vouchers Payable.

- ▶ Record the transaction.

STEP 4: Key the cash payment transactions for April, 2002 into the Cash Register. From the Banking menu choose the Use Register option. When the Select Account window appears, choose Cash.

- ▶ Key the date of the new voucher transaction.

- ▶ Key the Check Number.

- ▶ Key or select the Vendor.

- ▶ Key the amount of the check in the Payment column.

- ▶ Key or select Vouchers Payable in the Account field. If a discount is involved, click on the Split button. The split option allows you to enter a multi-part transaction. Key the discount amount as a negative number. The computer will make the offsetting entry to Cash.

- ▶ Key the Voucher Number in the Memo field.

- ▶ Record the transaction.

STEP 5: From the Memorized Reports list, display the following reports:

Vouchers Journal Report

Cash Payments Journal Report

Trial Balance Report

Schedule of Accounts Payable (Vendor Balance Summary)

PROBLEM 14-3B

Jane Hledik is owner of Hledik Lawn Supply. The following transactions occurred during April 2000. Hledik Lawn Supply uses a voucher register, a check register, and a general ledger. Unpaid vouchers are filed and listed at the end of the month. General ledger account balances on April 1 were: Cash, $5,189; and Supplies, $408.

Vouchers issued:

Date	Voucher No.	Issued To	Amount	Purpose	Terms
4/2	662	Brenner's	$600	April rent	
4/4	663	Lawn Care Wholesale	300	Merchandise	2/10, n/30
4/7	664	Southern Supply	128	Office supplies	
4/10	665	Clay's Chemicals	420	Merchandise	1/20, n/30
4/13	666	Mendel & Son	530	Merchandise	2/10, n/30
4/15	667	Payroll	950	Bimonthly payroll	
4/19	668	Lawn Care Wholesale	570	Merchandise	1/10, n/30
4/27	669	Southern Supply	99	Office supplies	
4/29	670	Lakeside Fertilizer	280	Merchandise	2/10, n/30
4/30	671	Payroll	950	Bimonthly payroll	

Checks issued:

Date	Check No.	Payee	Voucher No.	Amount
4/2	748	Brenner's	662	$600
4/7	749	Southern Supply	664	128
4/11	750	Lawn Care Wholesale	663	300
4/15	751	Payroll	667	950
4/20	752	Mendel & Son	666	530
4/30	753	Payroll	671	950

Follow the step-by-step instructions provided to solve the problem.

STEP 1:   **Start up the QuickBooks software.**

Choose QuickBooks Pro from the Start button.

STEP 2:   **Restore the Opening Balance data for Problem 14-3B.**

▶   From the File menu, choose Restore.

▶   When the Restore From window appears, select "14-03B.QBB" and click on Open.

▶   When the Restore To window appears, use the Save in option to select the folder in which you wish to store your QuickBooks files, key a file name, and click on Save.

The file name that you choose should identify the file as yours (14-03B Jane Doe). QuickBooks will add an extension of QBW.

▶   If the file already exists, you will get a caution message. You must key "YES" and click OK to overwrite an existing file.

STEP 3:   **Key the Voucher transactions for April, 2002 into the Vouchers Payable Register. From the Banking menu choose the Use Register option. When the Select Account window appears, choose Vouchers Payable.**

▶   Key the date of the new voucher transaction.

▶   Key the Voucher Number into the Number field.

▶   Key or select the Vendor.

▶   Calculate and enter the Due Date.

▶   Key the Voucher amount in the Billed column.

▶   Key the account to be debited into the Account field.

▶   The computer will make the offsetting entry to Vouchers Payable.

▶   Record the transaction.

STEP 4:   **Key the cash payment transactions for April, 2002 into the Cash Register. From the Banking menu choose the Use Register option. When the Select Account window appears, choose Cash.**

▶   Key the date of the new voucher transaction.

▶   Key the Check Number.

▶   Key or select the Vendor.

▶   Key the amount of the check in the Payment column.

▶   Key or select Vouchers Payable in the Account field. If a discount is involved, click on the Split button. The split option allows you to enter a multi-part transaction. Key the discount amount as a negative number. The computer will make the offsetting entry to Cash.

▶ Key the Voucher Number in the Memo field.

▶ Record the transaction.

STEP 5: From the Memorized Reports list, display the following reports:

Vouchers Journal Report

Cash Payments Journal Report

Schedule of Accounts Payable (Vendor Balance Summary)

General Ledger Report

Trial Balance Report

CHAPTER 14 MASTERY PROBLEM

Sunshine Flower Shop began operations in the month of July. The following transactions occurred during the first month of the business.

July 1   Purchased merchandise from Thorny Wholesale, $600. Voucher no. 1.

      2   Issued check no. 1 to Strongs Rental for July rent, $1,000. Voucher no. 2

      3   Purchased merchandise from Flowerbed, Inc., $470, terms 2/15, n/60, FOB shipping point. Voucher no. 3.

      7   Issued check no. 2 to Thorny Wholesale in partial payment for goods purchased on July 1, $300. Voucher no. 1. Issued new voucher nos. 4 and 5.

      9   Issued check no. 3 to Charlie's Trucking for shipping charges, $20. Voucher no. 6.

    15   Issued check no. 4 to Payroll for wages, $600. Voucher no. 7.

    16   Purchased merchandise from Petals Co., $377, terms 2/15, n/30. Voucher no. 8.

    17   Purchased merchandise from Weeds Plus, $436, terms 3/15, n/60. Voucher no. 9.

    18   Issued check no. 5 to Flowerbed, Inc., for goods purchased on July 3 less discount. Voucher no. 3.

    23   Purchased supplies from Staples Supply, $150. Voucher no. 10.

    25   Received a credit memo from Weeds Plus for returned merchandise that was purchased on July 17, $80.

    31   Issued check no. 6 to Petals Co. for goods purchased on July 16 less discount. Voucher no. 8.

    31   Issued check no. 7 to Payroll for wages, $600. Voucher no. 11.

The general ledger accounts are listed below. The $6,000 with which the Flower Shop began business is entered in the cash account. Only this account has a beginning balance.

Cash	101
Supplies	141
Vouchers Payable	202
Purchases	501
Purchases Returns and Allowances	501.1
Purchases Discounts	501.2
Freight-In	502
Wages Expense	511
Rent Expense	521

Follow the step-by-step instructions provided to solve the problem.

STEP 1:   Start up the QuickBooks software.

Choose QuickBooks Pro from the Start button.

STEP 2:   Restore the Opening Balance data for the Chapter 14 Mastery Problem.

▶ From the File menu, choose Restore.

▶ When the Restore From window appears, select "14 Mastery Problem.QBB" and click on Open.

▶ When the Restore To window appears, use the Save in option to select the folder in which you wish to store your QuickBooks files, key a file name, and click on Save.

The file name that you choose should identify the file as yours (14 Mastery Jane Doe). QuickBooks will add an extension of QBW.

▶ If the file already exists, you will get a caution message. You must key "YES" and click OK to overwrite an existing file.

STEP 3:   Key the Voucher transactions for July, 2002 into the Vouchers Payable Register. From the Banking menu choose the Use Register option. When the Select Account window appears, choose Vouchers Payable.

▶ Key the date of the new voucher transaction.

▶ Key the Voucher Number into the Number field.

▶ Key or select the Vendor.

▶ Calculate and enter the Due Date.

▶ Key the Voucher amount in the Billed column.

▶ Key the account to be debited into the Account field.

▶ The computer will make the offsetting entry to Vouchers Payable.

▶ Record the transaction.

Note: In the transactions narrative, you are directed to replace Voucher 1 (for $600) with Vouchers 4 and 5 for $300 each so that a partial payment of $300 can be made. With the QuickBooks software, it is not necessary to create the two new vouchers. You can simply make a partial payment of $300 when directed to do so.

STEP 4:   Key the cash payment transactions for July, 2002 into the Cash Register. From the Banking menu choose the Use Register option. When the Select Account window appears, choose Cash.

▶ Key the date of the new voucher transaction.

▶ Key the Check Number.

▶ Key or select the Vendor.

▶ Key the amount of the check in the Payment column.

▶ Key or select Vouchers Payable in the Account field. If a discount is involved, click on the Splits button. The split option allows you to enter a multi-part transaction. Key the discount amount as a negative number. The computer will make the offsetting entry to Cash.

▶ Key the Voucher Number in the Memo field.

▶ Record the transaction.

STEP 5:   Key the General Journal entry on July 25, 2002 to record the merchandise return.

STEP 6:   From the Memorized Reports list, display the following reports:

Vouchers Journal Report

Cash Payments Journal Report

General Journal Report

General Ledger Report

Schedule of Accounts Payable (Vendor Balance Summary)

PROBLEM 15-1A

The trial balance for the Seaside Kite Shop, a business owned by Joyce Kennington, is shown on the following page. Year-end adjustment information is as follows:

(a, b) Merchandise inventory costing $30,000 is on hand as of December 31, 2000.

(c) Supplies remaining at the end of the year, $2,700.

(d) Unexpired insurance on December 31, $2,900.

(e) Depreciation expense on the building for 2000, $5,000.

(f) Depreciation expense on the store equipment for 2000, $3,200.

(g) Unearned rent revenue as of December 31, $2,200.

(h) Wages earned but not paid as of December 31, $900.

Follow the step-by-step instructions below to complete the problem.

STEP 1:   **Start up the QuickBooks software.**

Choose QuickBooks Pro from the Start button.

STEP 2:   **Restore the Opening Balance data for Problem 15-1A.**

▶ **From the File menu, choose Restore.**

▶ **When the Restore From window appears, select "Problem 15-01A.QBB" and click on Open.**

▶ **When the Restore To window appears, use the Save in option to select the folder in which you wish to store your QuickBooks files, key a file name, and click on Save.**

The file name that you choose should identify the file as yours (15-01A Jane Doe). QuickBooks will add an extension of QBW.

▶ **If the file already exists, you will get a caution message. You must key "YES" and click OK to overwrite an existing file.**

STEP 3:   **Display the Trial Balance Report from the Memorized Reports list.**

STEP 4:   **From the Company menu, select the Make Journal Entry option and key the adjusting entries for December 31, 2002. The adjusting entries for merchandise inventory are shown in the General Journal Entry window in Figure 2.24 and Figure 2.25.**

Seaside Kite Shop
Trial Balance
December 31, 20 - -

ACCOUNT TITLE	DEBIT BALANCE					CREDIT BALANCE				
Cash	20	0	0	0	00					
Accounts Receivable	14	0	0	0	00					
Merchandise Inventory	25	0	0	0	00					
Supplies	8	0	0	0	00					
Prepaid Insurance	5	4	0	0	00					
Land	30	0	0	0	00					
Building	50	0	0	0	00					
Accumulated Depreciation—Building						20	0	0	0	00
Store Equipment	35	0	0	0	00					
Accumulated Depreciation—Store Equipment						14	0	0	0	00
Accounts Payable						9	6	0	0	00
Wages Payable										
Sales Tax Payable						5	9	0	0	00
Unearned Rent Revenue						8	9	0	0	00
Mortgage Payable						45	0	0	0	00
Joyce Kennington, Capital						65	4	1	0	00
Joyce Kennington, Drawing	26	0	0	0	00					
Income Summary										
Sales						118	0	0	0	00
Sales Returns and Allowances	1	7	0	0	00					
Rent Revenue										
Purchases	27	0	0	0	00					
Purchases Returns and Allowances						1	4	0	0	00
Purchases Discounts						1	8	0	0	00
Freight-In	2	1	0	0	00					
Wages Expense	32	0	0	0	00					
Advertising Expense	3	6	0	0	00					
Supplies Expense										
Telephone Expense	1	3	5	0	00					
Utilities Expense	8	0	0	0	00					
Insurance Expense										
Depreciation Expense —Building										
Depreciation Expense —Store Equipment										
Miscellaneous Expense		8	6	0	00					
	290	0	1	0	00	290	0	1	0	00

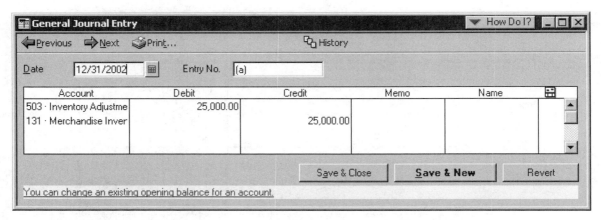

FIGURE 2.24 Merchandise Inventory Adjusting Entry in the General Journal Entry Window

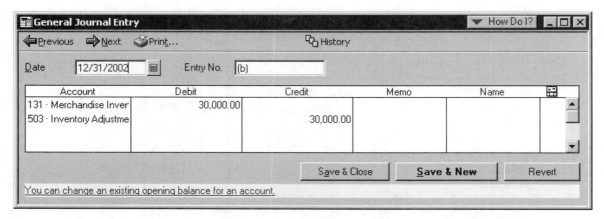

FIGURE 2.25 Merchandise Inventory Adjusting Entry in the General Journal Entry Window

Note: Key the letter for each adjusting entry in the Entry No. field. QuickBooks requires that the adjusting entry for Merchandise Inventory be made to Inventory Adjustment (Account No. 503) rather than to the Income Summary account.

STEP 5:   **From the Memorized Reports list, display the following reports:**

Adjusting Entries Journal Report

Income Statement Report

Balance Sheet Report

PROBLEM 15-2A

The trial balance for Cascade Bicycle Shop, a business owned by David Lamond, is shown on the following page. Year-end adjustment information is provided:

(a, b)   Merchandise inventory costing $22,000 is on hand as of December 31, 2000.

(c)   Supplies remaining at the end of the year, $2,400.

(d)   Unexpired insurance on December 31, $1,750.

Cascade Bicycle Shop
Trial Balance
December 31, 20 - -

ACCOUNT TITLE	DEBIT BALANCE					CREDIT BALANCE				
Cash	23	0	0	0	00					
Accounts Receivable	15	0	0	0	00					
Merchandise Inventory	31	0	0	0	00					
Supplies	7	2	0	0	00					
Prepaid Insurance	4	6	0	0	00					
Land	28	0	0	0	00					
Building	53	0	0	0	00					
Accumulated Depreciation—Building						17	0	0	0	00
Store Equipment	27	0	0	0	00					
Accumulated Depreciation—Store Equipment						9	0	0	0	00
Accounts Payable						3	8	0	0	00
Wages Payable										
Sales Tax Payable						3	0	5	0	00
Unearned Storage Revenue						5	6	0	0	00
Mortgage Payable						42	0	0	0	00
David Lamond, Capital						165	7	6	0	00
David Lamond, Drawing	33	0	0	0	00					
Income Summary										
Sales						51	0	0	0	00
Sales Returns and Allowances	2	4	0	0	00					
Storage Revenue										
Purchases	21	0	0	0	00					
Purchases Returns and Allowances						1	3	0	0	00
Purchases Discounts						1	9	0	0	00
Freight-In	1	8	0	0	00					
Wages Expense	35	0	0	0	00					
Advertising Expense	5	7	0	0	00					
Supplies Expense										
Telephone Expense	2	2	0	0	00					
Utilities Expense	9	6	0	0	00					
Insurance Expense										
Depreciation Expense —Building										
Depreciation Expense —Store Equipment										
Miscellaneous Expense		9	1	0	00					
	300	4	1	0	00	300	4	1	0	00

(e)   Depreciation expense on the building for 2000, $4,000.

(f)   Depreciation expense on the store equipment for 2000, $3,600.

(g)   Unearned storage revenue as of December 31, $1,950.

(h)   Wages earned but not paid as of December 31, $750.

In Problem 15-2A, you will enter the adjusting entries and display the financial statements for a merchandising business. Follow the steps listed below to complete the problem.

STEP 1:   Start up the QuickBooks software.

Choose QuickBooks Pro from the Start button.

STEP 2:   Restore the Opening Balance data for Problem 15-2A.

▶ **From the File menu, choose Restore.**

▶ **When the Restore From window appears, select "Problem 15-02A.QBB" and click on Open.**

▶ **When the Restore To window appears, use the Save in option to select the folder in which you wish to store your QuickBooks files, key a file name, and click on Save.**

The file name that you choose should identify the file as yours (15-02A Jane Doe). QuickBooks will add an extension of QBW.

▶ **If the file already exists, you will get a caution message. You must key "YES" and click OK to overwrite an existing file.**

STEP 3:   Display the Trial Balance Report from the Memorized Reports list.

STEP 4:   From the Company menu, select the Make Journal Entry option and key the adjusting entries for December 31, 2002.

Note: Key the letter for each adjusting entry in the Entry No. field. QuickBooks requires that the adjusting entry for Merchandise Inventory be made to Inventory Adjustment (Account No. 503) rather than to the Income Summary account.

STEP 5:   From the Memorized Reports list, display the following reports:

Adjusting Entries Journal Report

Income Statement Report

Balance Sheet Report

PROBLEM 15-1B

A trial balance for the Basket Corner, a business owned by Linda Palermo, is shown on the following page. Year-end adjustment information is provided:

(a, b) Merchandise inventory costing $24,000 is on hand as of December 31, 2000.

(c)   Supplies remaining at the end of the year, $2,100.

(d)   Unexpired insurance on December 31, $2,600.

(e)   Depreciation expense on the building for 2000, $5,300.

(f)   Depreciation expense on the store equipment for 2000, $3,800.

Basket Corner
Trial Balance
December 31, 20 - -

ACCOUNT TITLE	DEBIT BALANCE					CREDIT BALANCE				
Cash	25	0	0	0	00					
Accounts Receivable	8	1	0	0	00					
Merchandise Inventory	32	0	0	0	00					
Supplies	7	1	0	0	00					
Prepaid Insurance	3	6	0	0	00					
Land	40	0	0	0	00					
Building	45	0	0	0	00					
Accumulated Depreciation—Building						16	0	0	0	00
Store Equipment	27	0	0	0	00					
Accumulated Depreciation—Store Equipment						5	5	0	0	00
Accounts Payable						3	6	0	0	00
Wages Payable										
Sales Tax Payable						6	2	0	0	00
Unearned Decorating Revenue						6	3	0	0	00
Mortgage Payable						36	0	0	0	00
Linda Palermo, Capital						112	0	5	0	00
Linda Palermo, Drawing	31	0	0	0	00					
Income Summary										
Sales						125	0	0	0	00
Sales Returns and Allowances	2	6	0	0	00					
Decorating Revenue										
Purchases	38	0	0	0	00					
Purchases Returns and Allowances						2	2	0	0	00
Purchases Discounts						1	7	0	0	00
Freight-In	1	9	0	0	00					
Wages Expense	38	0	0	0	00					
Advertising Expense	4	2	0	0	00					
Supplies Expense										
Telephone Expense	1	8	7	0	00					
Utilities Expense	8	4	0	0	00					
Insurance Expense										
Depreciation Expense —Building										
Depreciation Expense —Store Equipment										
Miscellaneous Expense		7	8	0	00					
	314	5	5	0	00	314	5	5	0	00

(g)   Unearned decorating revenue as of December 31, $1,650.

(h)   Wages earned but not paid as of December 31, $750.

    In Problem 15-1B, you will enter the adjusting entries and display the financial statements for a merchandising business. Follow the steps listed below to complete the problem.

STEP 1:   **Start up the QuickBooks software.**

    Choose QuickBooks Pro from the Start button.

STEP 2:   **Restore the Opening Balance data for Problem 15-1B.**

▶   **From the File menu, choose Restore.**

▶   **When the Restore From window appears, select "Problem 15-01B.QBB" and click on Open.**

▶   **When the Restore To window appears, use the Save in option to select the folder in which you wish to store your QuickBooks files, key a file name, and click on Save.**

    The file name that you choose should identify the file as yours (15-01B Jane Doe). QuickBooks will add an extension of QBW.

▶   **If the file already exists, you will get a caution message. You must key "YES" and click OK to overwrite an existing file.**

STEP 3:   **Display the Trial Balance Report from the Memorized Reports list.**

STEP 4:   **From the Company menu, select the Make Journal Entry option and key the adjusting entries for December 31, 2002.**

    Note: Key the letter for each adjusting entry in the Entry No. field. QuickBooks requires that the adjusting entry for Merchandise Inventory be made to Inventory Adjustment (Account No. 503) rather than to the Income Summary account.

STEP 5:   **From the Memorized Reports list, display the following reports:**

    Adjusting Entries Journal Report

    Income Statement Report

    Balance Sheet Report

PROBLEM 15-2B

The trial balance for Oregon Bike Company, a business owned by Craig Moody, is shown on the following page. Year-end adjustment information is provided:

(a, b)   Merchandise inventory costing $26,000 is on hand as of December 31, 2000.

(c)   Supplies remaining at the end of the year, $2,500.

(d)   Unexpired insurance on December 31, $1,820.

(e)   Depreciation expense on the building for 2000, $6,400.

(f)   Depreciation expense on the store equipment for 2000, $2,800.

(g)   Unearned rent revenue as of December 31, $2,350.

(h)   Wages earned but not paid as of December 31, $1,100.

Oregon Bike Company
Trial Balance
December 31, 20 - -

ACCOUNT TITLE	DEBIT BALANCE					CREDIT BALANCE				
Cash	27	0	0	0	00					
Accounts Receivable	12	0	0	0	00					
Merchandise Inventory	39	0	0	0	00					
Supplies	6	2	0	0	00					
Prepaid Insurance	5	8	0	0	00					
Land	32	0	0	0	00					
Building	58	0	0	0	00					
Accumulated Depreciation—Building						27	0	0	0	00
Store Equipment	31	0	0	0	00					
Accumulated Depreciation—Store Equipment						14	0	0	0	00
Accounts Payable						4	9	0	0	00
Wages Payable										
Sales Tax Payable						2	9	0	0	00
Unearned Rent Revenue						6	1	0	0	00
Mortgage Payable						49	0	0	0	00
Craig Moody, Capital						169	5	0	0	00
Craig Moody, Drawing	36	0	0	0	00					
Income Summary										
Sales						58	0	0	0	00
Sales Returns and Allowances	3	3	0	0	00					
Rent Revenue										
Purchases	19	0	0	0	00					
Purchases Returns and Allowances							9	0	0	00
Purchases Discounts						1	4	5	0	00
Freight-In		8	0	0	00					
Wages Expense	47	0	0	0	00					
Advertising Expense	6	2	0	0	00					
Supplies Expense										
Telephone Expense	1	8	6	0	00					
Utilities Expense	8	1	0	0	00					
Insurance Expense										
Depreciation Expense —Building										
Depreciation Expense —Store Equipment										
Miscellaneous Expense		4	9	0	00					
	333	7	5	0	00	333	7	5	0	00

In Problem 15-2B, you will enter the adjusting entries and display the financial statements for a merchandising business. Follow the steps listed below to complete the problem.

STEP 1:   Start up the QuickBooks software.

Choose QuickBooks Pro from the Start button.

STEP 2:   Restore the Opening Balance data for Problem 15-2B.

▶ **From the File menu, choose Restore.**

▶ **When the Restore From window appears, select "Problem 15-02B.QBB" and click on Open.**

▶ **When the Restore To window appears, use the Save in option to select the folder in which you wish to store your QuickBooks files, key a file name, and click on Save.**

The file name that you choose should identify the file as yours (15-02B Jane Doe). QuickBooks will add an extension of QBW.

▶ **If the file already exists, you will get a caution message. You must key "YES" and click OK to overwrite an existing file.**

STEP 3:   Display the Trial Balance Report from the Memorized Reports list.

STEP 4:   From the Company menu, select the Make Journal Entry option and key the adjusting entries for December 31, 2002.

Note: Key the letter for each adjusting entry in the Entry No. field. QuickBooks requires that the adjusting entry for Merchandise Inventory be made to Inventory Adjustment (Account No. 503) rather than to the Income Summary account.

STEP 5:   From the Memorized Reports list, display the following reports:

Adjusting Entries Journal Report

Income Statement Report

Balance Sheet Report

CHAPTER 15 MASTERY PROBLEM

John Neff owns and operates the Waikiki Surf Shop. A year-end trial balance is shown on the following page. Year-end adjustment data for the Waikiki Surf Shop is as follows:

(a, b)   A physical count shows merchandise inventory costing $45,000 on hand as of December 31, 2000.

(c)   Supplies remaining at the end of the year, $600.

(d)   Unexpired insurance on December 31, $900.

(e)   Depreciation expense on the building for 2000, $6,000.

(f)   Depreciation expense on the store equipment for 2000, $4,500.

(g)   Wages earned but not paid as of December 31, $675.

(h)   Unearned boat rental revenue as of December 31, $3,000.

In the Chapter 15 Mastery Problem, you will enter the adjusting entries and display the financial statements for a merchandising business. Follow the steps listed below to complete the problem.

STEP 1:   Start up the QuickBooks software.

Choose QuickBooks Pro from the Start button.

Waikiki Surf Shop
Trial Balance
December 31, 20 - -

ACCOUNT TITLE	DEBIT BALANCE					CREDIT BALANCE				
Cash	30	0	0	0	00					
Accounts Receivable	22	5	0	0	00					
Merchandise Inventory	57	0	0	0	00					
Supplies	2	7	0	0	00					
Prepaid Insurance	3	6	0	0	00					
Land	15	0	0	0	00					
Building	135	0	0	0	00					
Accumulated Depreciation—Building						24	0	0	0	00
Store Equipment	75	0	0	0	00					
Accumulated Depreciation—Store Equipment						22	5	0	0	00
Notes Payable						7	5	0	0	00
Accounts Payable						15	0	0	0	00
Wages Payable										
Unearned Boat Rental Revenue						33	0	0	0	00
John Neff, Capital						233	7	0	0	00
John Neff, Drawing	30	0	0	0	00					
Income Summary										
Sales						300	7	5	0	00
Sales Returns and Allowances	1	8	0	0	00					
Boat Rental Revenue										
Purchases	157	5	0	0	00					
Purchases Returns and Allowances						1	2	0	0	00
Purchases Discounts						1	5	0	0	00
Freight-In		4	5	0	00					
Wages Expense	63	0	0	0	00					
Advertising Expense	11	2	5	0	00					
Supplies Expense										
Telephone Expense	5	2	5	0	00					
Utilities Expense	18	0	0	0	00					
Insurance Expense										
Depreciation Expense —Building										
Depreciation Expense —Store Equipment										
Miscellaneous Expense	10	8	7	5	00					
Interest Expense		2	2	5	00					
	639	1	5	0	00	639	1	5	0	00

STEP 2:   Restore the Opening Balance data for the Chapter 15 Mastery Problem.

▶   From the File menu, choose Restore.

▶   When the Restore From window appears, select "15 Mastery Problem.QBB" and click on Open.

▶   When the Restore To window appears, use the Save in option to select the folder in which you wish to store your QuickBooks files, key a file name, and click on Save.

The file name that you choose should identify the file as yours (15 Mastery Jane Doe). QuickBooks will add an extension of QBW.

▶   If the file already exists, you will get a caution message. You must key "YES" and click OK to overwrite an existing file.

STEP 3:   Display the Trial Balance Report from the Memorized Reports list.

STEP 4:   From the Company menu, select the Make Journal Entry option and key the adjusting entries for December 31, 2002.

Note: Key the letter for each adjusting entry in the Entry No. field, e.g. (a), (b). QuickBooks requires that the adjusting entry for Merchandise Inventory be made to Inventory Adjustment (Account No. 503) rather than to the Income Summary account.

STEP 5:   From the Memorized Reports list, display the following reports:

Adjusting Entries Journal Report

Income Statement Report

Balance Sheet Report

CHAPTER 16 DEMONSTRATION PROBLEM

Tom McKinney owns and operates McK's Home Electronics. He has a store where he sells and repairs televisions and stereo equipment. A completed worksheet for 2000 is provided on page 127. McKinney made a $20,000 additional investment during 2000. The current portion of Mortgage Payable is $1,000. Credit sales for 2000 were $200,000, and the balance of Accounts Receivable on January 1 was $26,000.

In the Chapter 16 Demonstration Problem, you will enter the adjusting entries and display the financial statements for a merchandising business. After the financial statements have been prepared, you will close out the accounting period, and enter the reversing entries.

Follow the steps listed to complete the problem.

STEP 1:   Start up the QuickBooks software.

Choose QuickBooks Pro from the Start button.

STEP 2:   Restore the Opening Balance data for the Chapter 16 Demonstration Problem.

▶   From the File menu, choose Restore.

▶   When the Restore From window appears, select "16 Demonstration Problem.QBB" and click on Open.

▶   When the Restore To window appears, use the Save in option to select the folder in which you wish to store your QuickBooks files, key a file name, and click on Save.

The file name that you choose should identify the file as yours (16 Demo Jane Doe) QuickBooks will add an extension of QBW.

▶ If the file already exists, you will get a caution message. You must key "YES" and click OK to overwrite an existing file.

STEP 3: **Display the Trial Balance Report from the Memorized Reports list.**

STEP 4: **From the Company menu, select the Make Journal Entry option and key the adjusting entries for December 31, 2002.**

Note: Key the letter for each adjusting entry in the Entry No. field. QuickBooks requires that the adjusting entry for Merchandise Inventory be made to Inventory Adjustment (Account No. 503) rather than to the Income Summary account.

STEP 5: **From the Memorized Reports list, display the following reports:**

Adjusting Entries Journal Report

Income Statement Report

Balance Sheet Report

STEP 6: **Key the entry for December 31, 2002 to close the drawing account to capital. Key Clo.Ent. as the Entry No. The closing entry in the General Journal Entry window is shown in Figure 2.26.**

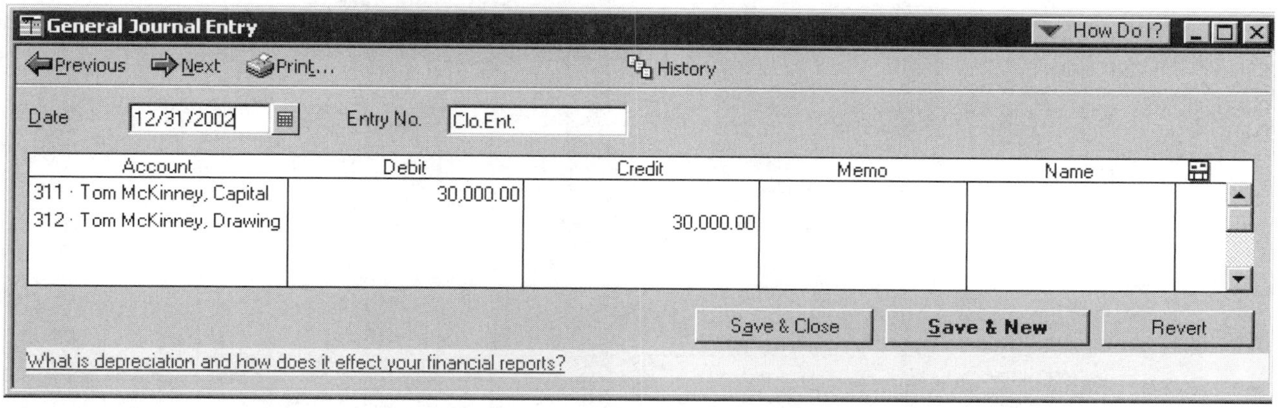

FIGURE 2.26 Closing Entry in the General Journal Entry Window

STEP 7: **Display a Post-Closing Trial Balance Report from the Memorized Reports list.**

Note: It isn't necessary to make closing entries to close out revenue and expense accounts. QuickBooks controls the process by date. Notice that the trial balance report as of January 1, 2003 (the beginning of a new fiscal period) has the revenue and expense accounts closed to Capital.

STEP 8: **Key the reversing entry in the General Journal for January 1, 2003. Key Rev. Ent. as the Entry No.**

STEP 9: **Display the Reversing Entries Report from the Memorized Reports list.**

See the Solution section of this workbook for the solution to this demonstration problem.

PROBLEM 16-1A

Ellis Fabric Store trial balance as of December 31, 2000 is shown on the following page.

At the end of the year, the following adjustments need to be made:

(a, b)   Merchandise Inventory as of December 31, $28,900.

ACCOUNT TITLE	ACCOUNT NO.	DEBIT BALANCE					CREDIT BALANCE				
Cash		28	0	0	0	00					
Accounts Receivable		14	2	0	0	00					
Merchandise Inventory		33	0	0	0	00					
Supplies		1	6	0	0	00					
Prepaid Insurance			9	0	0	00					
Equipment		6	6	0	0	00					
Accumulated Depreciation—Equipment							1	0	0	0	00
Accounts Payable							16	6	2	0	00
Wages Payable											
Sales Tax Payable								8	5	0	00
W. P. Ellis, Capital							71	2	0	0	00
W. P. Ellis, Drawing		21	6	1	0	00					
Income Summary											
Sales							78	5	0	0	00
Sales Returns and Allowances		1	8	5	0	00					
Interest Revenue							1	2	0	0	00
Purchases		41	5	0	0	00					
Purchases Returns and Allowances							1	8	0	0	00
Purchases Discounts								8	3	0	00
Freight-In			6	6	0	00					
Wages Expense		14	8	8	0	00					
Advertising Expense			8	1	0	00					
Supplies Expense											
Telephone Expense		1	2	1	0	00					
Utilities Expense		3	2	4	0	00					
Insurance Expense											
Depreciation Expense—Equipment											
Miscellaneous Expense			9	2	0	00					
Interest Expense		1	0	2	0	00					
		172	0	0	0	00	172	0	0	0	00

(c)   Unused supplies on hand, $1,350.

(d)   Insurance expired, $300.

(e)   Depreciation expense for the year, $500.

(f)   Wages earned but not paid (Wages Payable), $480.

In Problem 16-1A, you will enter the adjusting entries and display the financial statements for a merchandising business. After the financial statements have been prepared, you will close out the accounting period and enter the reversing entries.

Follow the steps listed to complete the problem.

STEP 1:   Start up the QuickBooks software.

Choose QuickBooks Pro from the Start button.

STEP 2:   Restore the Opening Balance data for Problem 16-1A.

▶   **From the File menu, choose Restore.**

▶   **When the Restore From window appears, select "Problem 16-01A.QBB" and click on Open.**

▶   **When the Restore To window appears, use the Save in option to select the folder in which you wish to store your QuickBooks files, key a file name, and click on Save.**

The file name that you choose should identify the file as yours (16-01A Jane Doe). QuickBooks will add an extension of QBW.

▶   **If the file already exists, you will get a caution message. You must key "YES" and click OK to overwrite an existing file.**

STEP 3:   Display the Trial Balance Report from the Memorized Reports list.

STEP 4:   From the Company menu, select the Make Journal Entry option and key the adjusting entries for December 31, 2002.

Note: Key the letter for each adjusting entry in the Entry No. field. QuickBooks requires that the adjusting entry for Merchandise Inventory be made to Inventory Adjustment (Account No. 503) rather than to the Income Summary account.

STEP 5:   From the Memorized Reports list, display the following reports:

Adjusting Entries Journal Report

Income Statement Report

Balance Sheet Report

STEP 6:   Key the entry for January 1, 2003 to close the drawing account to capital. Key Clo.Ent. as the Entry No.

STEP 7:   Display a Post-Closing Trial Balance Report from the Memorized Reports list.

Note: It isn't necessary to make closing entries to close out revenue and expense accounts. QuickBooks controls the process by date. Notice that the trial balance report as of January 1, 2003 (the beginning of a new fiscal period) has the revenue and expense accounts closed to Capital.

STEP 8:   Key the reversing entry in the General Journal for January 1, 2003. Key Rev. Ent. as the Entry No.

STEP 9:   Display the Reversing Entries Report from the Memorized Reports list.

PROBLEM 16-1B

The trial balance for Darby Kite Store as of December 31, 2000 is shown on the following page.
At the end of the year, the following adjustments need to be made:

(a, b)   Merchandise inventory as of December 31, $23,600.

(c)   Unused supplies on hand, $1,050.

(d)   Insurance expired, $250.

(e)   Depreciation expense for the year, $400.

(f)   Wages earned but not paid (Wages Payable), $360.

In Problem 16-1B, you will enter the adjusting entries and display the financial statements for a merchandising business. After the financial statements have been prepared, you will close out the accounting period, and enter the reversing entries.

Follow the steps listed to complete the problem.

STEP 1:   **Start up the QuickBooks software.**

Choose QuickBooks Pro from the Start button.

STEP 2:   **Restore the Opening Balance data for Problem 16-1B.**

▶   **From the File menu, choose Restore.**

▶   **When the Restore From window appears, select "Problem 16-01B.QBB" and click on Open.**

▶   **When the Restore To window appears, use the Save in option to select the folder in which you wish to store your QuickBooks files, key a file name, and click on Save.**

The file name that you choose should identify the file as yours (16-01B Jane Doe). QuickBooks will add an extension of QBW.

▶   **If the file already exists, you will get a caution message. You must key "YES" and click OK to overwrite an existing file.**

STEP 3:   **Display the Trial Balance Report from the Memorized Reports list.**

STEP 4:   **From the Company menu, select the Make Journal Entry option and key the adjusting entries for December 31, 2002.**

Note: Key the letter for each adjusting entry in the Entry No. field. QuickBooks requires that the adjusting entry for Merchandise Inventory be made to Inventory Adjustment (Account No. 503) rather than to the Income Summary account.

STEP 5:   **From the Memorized Reports list, display the following reports:**

Adjusting Entries Journal Report

Income Statement Report

Balance Sheet Report

STEP 6:   **Key the entry for January 1, 2003 to close the drawing account to capital. Key Clo.Ent. as the Entry No.**

STEP 7:   **Display a Post-Closing Trial Balance Report from the Memorized Reports list.**

Note: It isn't necessary to make closing entries to close out revenue and expense accounts. QuickBooks controls the process by date. Notice that the trial balance report as of January 1, 2003 (the beginning of a new fiscal period) has the revenue and expense accounts closed to Capital.

Darby Kite Store
Trial Balance
For Year Ended December 31, 20 - -

ACCOUNT TITLE	ACCOUNT NO.	DEBIT BALANCE					CREDIT BALANCE				
Cash		11	7	0	0	00					
Accounts Receivable		11	2	0	0	00					
Merchandise Inventory		25	0	0	0	00					
Supplies		1	2	0	0	00					
Prepaid Insurance			8	0	0	00					
Equipment		5	4	0	0	00					
Accumulated Depreciation—Equipment								8	0	0	00
Accounts Payable							7	6	0	0	00
Wages Payable											
Sales Tax Payable								2	5	0	00
M. D. Akins, Capital							50	0	0	0	00
M. D. Akins, Drawing		10	5	0	0	00					
Income Summary											
Sales							57	9	9	0	00
Sales Returns and Allowances		1	4	5	0	00					
Purchases		34	5	0	0	00					
Purchases Returns and Allowances							1	1	0	0	00
Purchases Discounts								6	3	0	00
Freight-In			3	6	0	00					
Wages Expense		10	8	8	0	00					
Advertising Expense			7	4	0	00					
Supplies Expense											
Telephone Expense		1	1	0	0	00					
Utilities Expense		2	3	0	0	00					
Insurance Expense											
Depreciation Expense—Equipment											
Miscellaneous Expense			3	2	0	00					
Interest Expense			9	2	0	00					
		118	3	7	0	00	118	3	7	0	00

STEP 8:   Key the reversing entry in the General Journal for January 1, 2003. Key Rev. Ent. as the Entry No.

STEP 9:   Display the Reversing Entries Report from the Memorized Reports list.

CHAPTER 16 MASTERY PROBLEM

In the Chapter 16 Mastery Problem, you will enter the adjusting entries and display the financial statements for a merchandising business. After the financial statements have been prepared, you will close out the accounting period and enter the reversing entries. Refer to the work sheet on the next page for adjusting entry information.

Follow the steps listed to complete the problem.

STEP 1:   **Start up the QuickBooks software.**
           Choose QuickBooks Pro from the Start button.

STEP 2:   **Restore the Opening Balance data for the Chapter 16 Mastery Problem.**

▶ **From the File menu, choose Restore.**

▶ **When the Restore From window appears, select "16 Mastery Problem.QBB" and click on Open.**

▶ **When the Restore To window appears, use the Save in option to select the folder in which you wish to store your QuickBooks files, key a file name, and click on Save.**
    The file name that you choose should identify the file as yours (16 Mastery Jane Doe). QuickBooks will add an extension of QBW.

▶ **If the file already exists, you will get a caution message. You must key "YES" and click OK to overwrite an existing file.**

STEP 3:   **Display the Trial Balance Report from the Memorized Reports list.**

STEP 4:   **From the Company menu, select the Make Journal Entry option and key the adjusting entries for December 31, 2002.**
           Note: Key the letter for each adjusting entry in the Entry No. field. QuickBooks requires that the adjusting entry for Merchandise Inventory be made to Inventory Adjustment (Account No. 503) rather than to the Income Summary account.

STEP 5:   **From the Memorized Reports list, display the following reports:**
           Adjusting Entries Journal Report
           Income Statement Report
           Balance Sheet Report

STEP 6:   **Key the entry for January 1, 2003 to close the drawing account to capital. Key Clo.Ent. as the Entry No.**

STEP 7:   **Display a Post-Closing Trial Balance Report from the Memorized Reports list.**
           Note: It isn't necessary to make closing entries to close out revenue and expense accounts. QuickBooks controls the process by date. Notice that the trial balance report as of January 1, 2003 (the beginning of a new fiscal period) has the revenue and expense accounts closed to Capital.

STEP 8:   **Key the reversing entry in the General Journal for January 1, 2003. Key Rev. Ent. as the Entry No.**

STEP 9:   **Display the Reversing Entries Report from the Memorized Reports list.**

Dominique's Doll House
Work Sheet
For Year Ended December 31, 20-3

#	Account Title	Trial Balance Debit	Trial Balance Credit	Adjustments Debit	Adjustments Credit	Adjusted Trial Balance Debit	Adjusted Trial Balance Credit	Income Statement Debit	Income Statement Credit	Balance Sheet Debit	Balance Sheet Credit
1	Cash	5 2 0 0 00				5 2 0 0 00				5 2 0 0 00	
2	Accounts Receivable	3 2 0 0 00				3 2 0 0 00				3 2 0 0 00	
3	Merchandise Inventory	22 3 0 0 00		(b) 24 6 0 0 00	(a) 22 3 0 0 00	24 6 0 0 00				24 6 0 0 00	
4	Office Supplies	8 0 0 00			(c) 6 0 0 00	2 0 0 00				2 0 0 00	
5	Prepaid Insurance	1 2 0 0 00			(d) 4 0 0 00	8 0 0 00				8 0 0 00	
6	Store Equipment	85 0 0 0 00				85 0 0 0 00				85 0 0 0 00	
7	Accum. Depr.—Store Equipment		15 0 0 0 00		(e) 5 0 0 0 00		20 0 0 0 00				20 0 0 0 00
8	Notes Payable		6 0 0 0 00				6 0 0 0 00				6 0 0 0 00
9	Accounts Payable		5 5 0 0 00				5 5 0 0 00				5 5 0 0 00
10	Wages Payable				(g) 2 0 0 00		2 0 0 00				2 0 0 00
11	Sales Tax Payable		8 5 0 00				8 5 0 00				8 5 0 00
12	Unearned Rent Revenue		1 0 0 0 00	(f) 7 0 0 00			3 0 0 00				3 0 0 00
13	Long-Term Note Payable		10 0 0 0 00				10 0 0 0 00				10 0 0 0 00
14	Dominique Fouque, Capital		75 8 0 0 00				75 8 0 0 00				75 8 0 0 00
15	Dominique Fouque, Drawing	21 0 0 0 00				21 0 0 0 00				21 0 0 0 00	
16	Income Summary			(a) 22 3 0 0 00	(b) 24 6 0 0 00	22 3 0 0 00	24 6 0 0 00	22 3 0 0 00	24 6 0 0 00		
17	Sales		130 5 0 0 00				130 5 0 0 00		130 5 0 0 00		
18	Sales Returns and Allowances	9 0 0 0 00				9 0 0 0 00		9 0 0 0 00			
19	Rent Revenue		25 0 0 0 00		(f) 7 0 0 00		25 7 0 0 00		25 7 0 0 00		
20	Purchases	72 0 0 0 00				72 0 0 0 00		72 0 0 0 00			
21	Purchases Discounts		7 5 0 00				7 5 0 00		7 5 0 00		
22	Freight-In	1 2 0 0 00				1 2 0 0 00		1 2 0 0 00			
23	Wages Expense	42 0 0 0 00		(g) 2 0 0 00		42 2 0 0 00		42 2 0 0 00			
24	Rent Expense	6 0 0 0 00				6 0 0 0 00		6 0 0 0 00			
25	Office Supplies Expense			(c) 6 0 0 00		6 0 0 00		6 0 0 00			
26	Telephone Expense	1 5 0 0 00				1 5 0 0 00		1 5 0 0 00			
27	Utilities Expense	7 6 0 0 00				7 6 0 0 00		7 6 0 0 00			
28	Insurance Expense			(d) 4 0 0 00		4 0 0 00		4 0 0 00			
29	Depr. Expense—Store Equipment			(e) 5 0 0 0 00		5 0 0 0 00		5 0 0 0 00			
30	Interest Expense	5 0 0 0 00				5 0 0 0 00		5 0 0 0 00			
31		270 4 0 0 00	270 4 0 0 00	53 8 0 0 00	53 8 0 0 00	300 2 0 0 00	300 2 0 0 00	160 2 0 0 00	181 5 5 0 00	140 0 0 0 00	118 6 5 0 00
32	Net Income							21 3 5 0 00			21 3 5 0 00
33								181 5 5 0 00	181 5 5 0 00	140 0 0 0 00	140 0 0 0 00

SECTION 3

Setting Up a New Company

This Section describes the process of setting up a new company. This process varies greatly depending on the size of the company as well as the type of company being setup. There are significant differences between how a service company, retail, or manufacturing company are setup. In this Section you will setup the Westside Lawn Service.

WESTSIDE LAWN SERVICE SETUP

As you complete this activity, you will complete the initial setup tasks, enter the chart of accounts, and establish the opening balances for Westside Law Service.

STEP 1:   **From the File Menu, choose the New option.**

The Easy Step Interview wizard shown in Figure 3.1 will appear. This QuickBooks interview process will lead you through the setup.

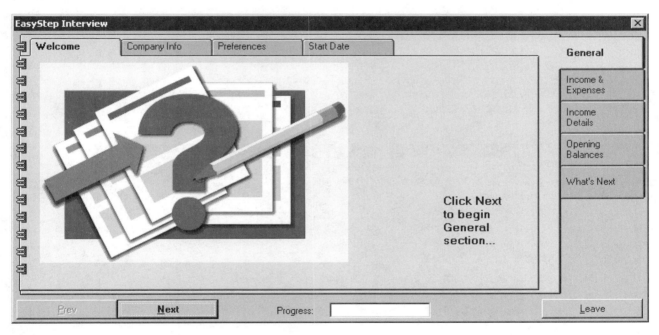

FIGURE 3.1 Easy Step Interview Window

STEP 2:   **Continue to click the Next button and read the Welcome screens as they appear until the Company Information screen shown in Figure 3.2 on the following page appears. Key "Westside Lawn Service" into both fields and click Next.**

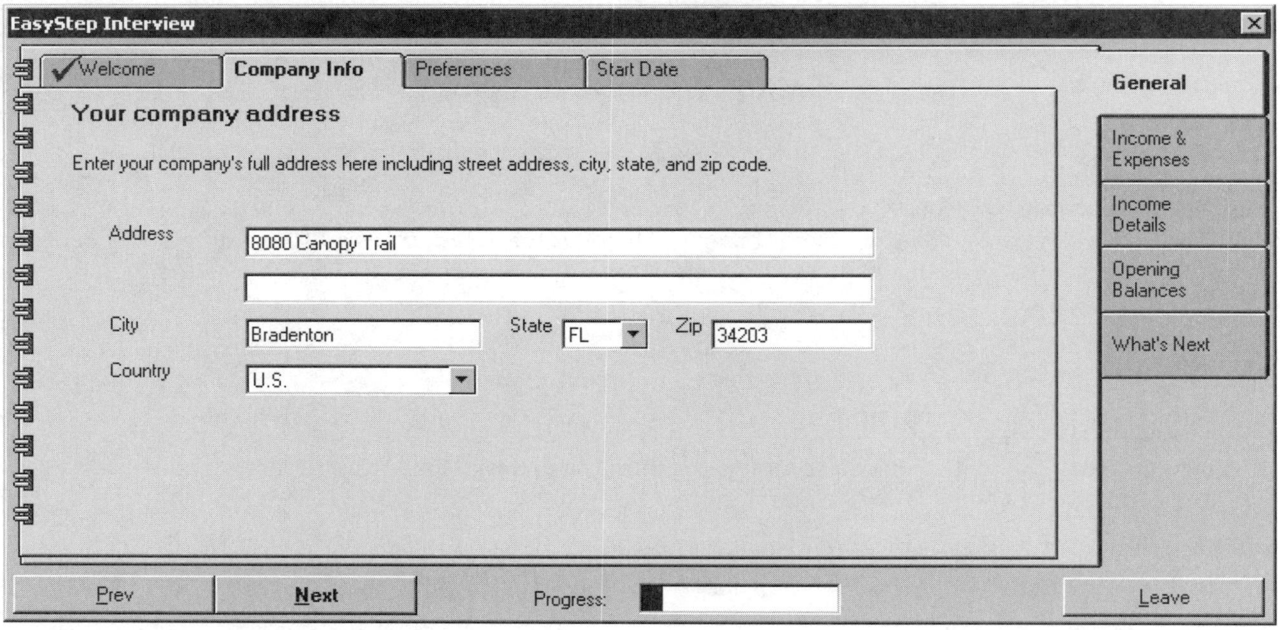

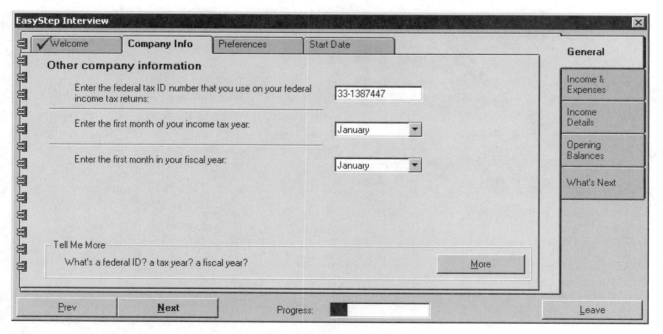

FIGURE 3.2 Company Information Window

STEP 3:   **Key the following address and click on Next.**

> 8080 Canopy Trail
> Bradenton, FL   34203

STEP 4:   **Key a Federal Tax ID number of 33-1387447 and starting month of January as illustrated in Figure 3.3 and click Next.**

FIGURE 3.3 Other Company Information (Federal Tax ID and Starting Month)

STEP 5: When the Company Income Tax form selection window appears, leave the drop-list selection at None and click Next.

STEP 6: When the Select Type of Business window shown in Figure 3.4 appears, select "Service Business" and click Next.

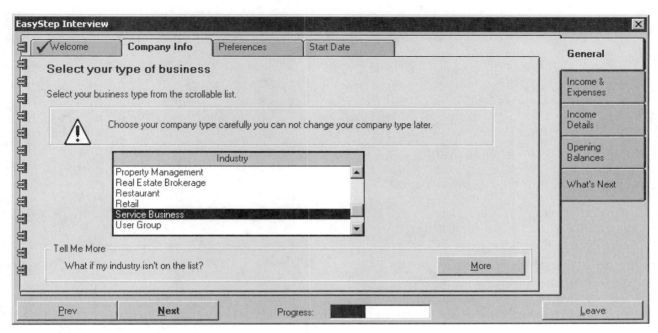

FIGURE 3.4 Select Type of Business Window

STEP 7: Click Next several times until the "Save As" window shown in Figure 3.5 appears. Choose the folder and file name where you would like to store your data file and click on Save.

FIGURE 3.5 Save As Window

STEP 8: When the Income and Expense accounts window shown in Figure 3.6 appears, choose the "No, I'd like to create my own" option and click Next.

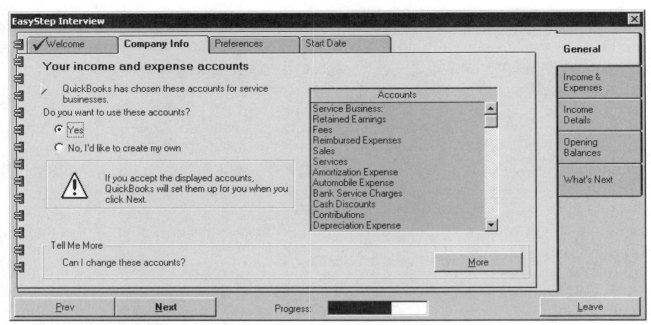

FIGURE 3.6 Income and Expense Accounts Window

STEP 9: When asked how many people beside yourself will access your company, choose 0 and click Next.

STEP 10: Continue to click Next until the Inventory screen shown in Figure 3.7 appears. Choose the "No" option and click Next.

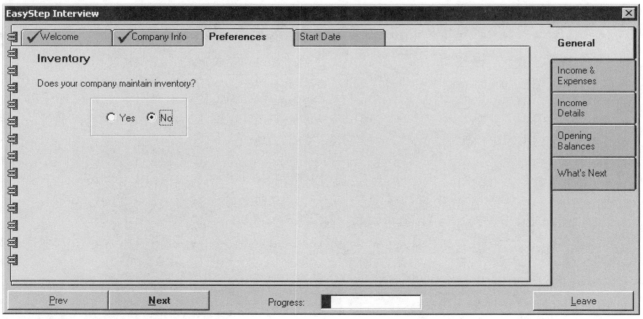

FIGURE 3.7 Inventory Window

STEP 11: When asked if you collect sales tax from your customers, respond "No" and click Next.

STEP 12: When asked to choose an invoice format, choose "Service" and click Next.

STEP 13: When asked if you wish to use the Payroll feature, choose "No" and click Next.

STEP 14: When asked if you prepare written or verbal estimates, respond "No" and click Next.

STEP 15: When asked if you wish to track the time your employees spend on each job, respond "No" and click Next.

STEP 16: When asked if you wish to use classes, respond "No" and click Next.

STEP 17: When asked how you wish to handle bills and payments, choose the "Enter the bills first and then enter the payments later" option and click Next.

STEP 18: When the Reminders list screen appears, choose the "When I ask for it" option and click Next.

STEP 19: When the accrual or cash based reporting window appears, choose the Accrual-based reports option and click Next.

STEP 20: Click Next until the Start Date window shown in Figure 3.8 appears. Enter a Start Date of January 1, 2002 and click Next.

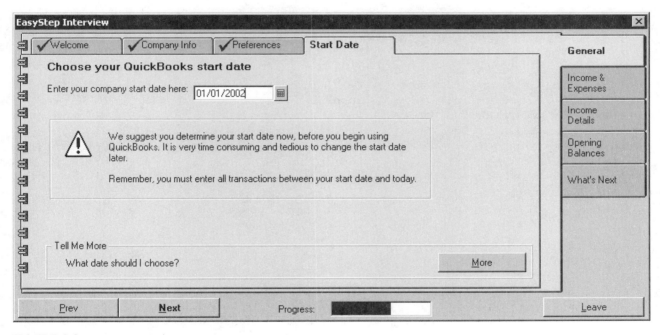

FIGURE 3.8 Start Date Window

STEP 21: Click on the Leave button.

STEP 22: From the Edit menu, choose Preferences. When the Preferences window shown in Figure 3.9 on the following page appears, click on the Accounting icon, click on the Company Preferences tab, and click the Use Account Numbers check box. Click Ok to record the data.

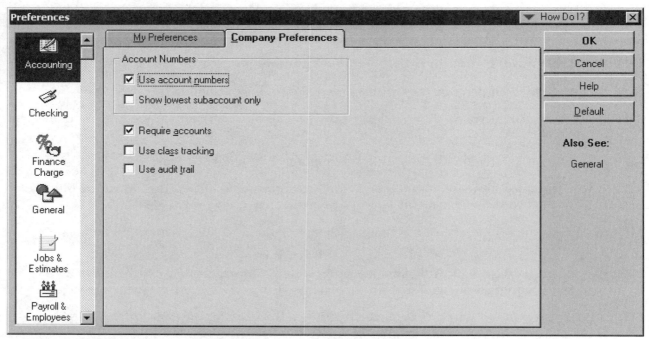

FIGURE 3.9 Company Preferences Window

STEP 23: From the Lists menu, choose the Chart of Accounts option. When the Chart of Accounts window shown in Figure 3.10 appears, click on Accounts, then choose New.

Acct. No.	Type	Title	Debit	Credit
1110	Bank	Cash	5960.48	
1130	Other Current Asset	Supplies	1245.95	
1140	Other Current Asset	Prepaid Insurance	397.00	
1510	Fixed Asset	Office Equipment	12051.15	
1511	Fixed Asset	Accum. Depr.—Ofc. Equip.		6121.25
1550	Fixed Asset	Lawn Equipment	34024.10	
1551	Fixed Asset	Accum. Depr.—Lawn Equip.		8101.10
2110	Other Current Liability	Notes Payable		15126.64
3110	Equity	Leonard Filter, Capital		37401.65
3120	Equity	Leonard Filter, Drawing	33276.87	
4110	Income	Lawn Service Fees		74451.97
5110	Expense	Rent Expense	16940.00	
5120	Expense	Salary Expense	19450.00	
5130	Expense	Supplies Expense		
5140	Expense	Utilities Expense	6761.61	
5150	Expense	Depr. Exp.—Office Equip.	3862.05	
5160	Expense	Depr. Exp.—Lawn Equip.	4590.00	
5170	Expense	Advertising Expense	1834.00	
5180	Expense	Insurance Expense		
5210	Expense	Miscellaneous Expense	809.40	

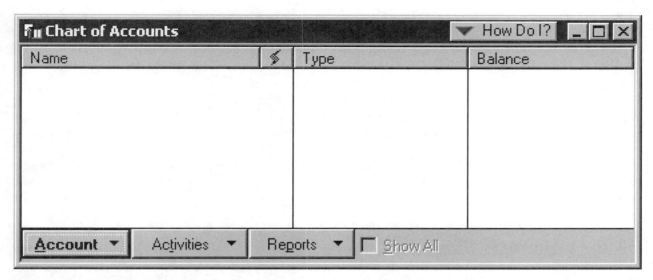

FIGURE 3.10 Chart of Accounts Window

STEP 24: Enter the chart of accounts and opening balances. The first entry to record the Cash
account is shown in Figure 3.11.

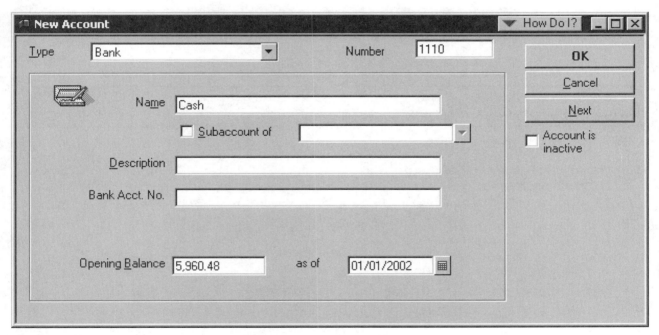

FIGURE 3.11 New Account Window

▶ Select "Bank" as the Type of account.
▶ Key 1110 as the account number.
▶ Key "Cash" as the account name.
▶ Tab to the Opening Balance and Key 5960.48.

Note: The Opening Balance field will not appear for income and expense accounts. The process for keying these account balances is identified in Step 25. When you enter the balance for the accumulated depreciation accounts and the drawing account, key these balances as negative numbers.

▶ **Key an As of date of 01/01/2002.**

▶ **Click on Ok to record the account.**

Notice that when the Chart of Accounts window shown in Figure 3.12 appears, it includes an additional entry for Account Number 3000, Opening Balance Equity with a balance of 5960.48. This is an equity account automatically established and maintained by QuickBooks. QuickBooks will always keep the accounting system in balance by adjusting this account balance. Each time you add an additional account balance, QuickBooks will adjust this balance. Once you have all your accounts and balances entered, this balance should be zero. If it is not, your accounting system is out of balance by the amount shown in the Opening Balance Equity account.

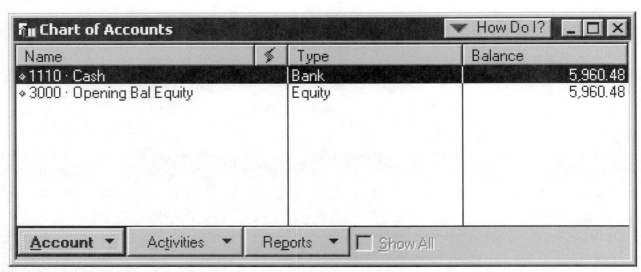

FIGURE 3.12 Chart of Accounts Window

STEP 25: To enter the income and expense accounts, double-click on the Opening Balances Equity account from the Chart of Accounts window. When the Opening Balance Equity register shown in Figure 3.13 appears, key each of the expense and revenue accounts.

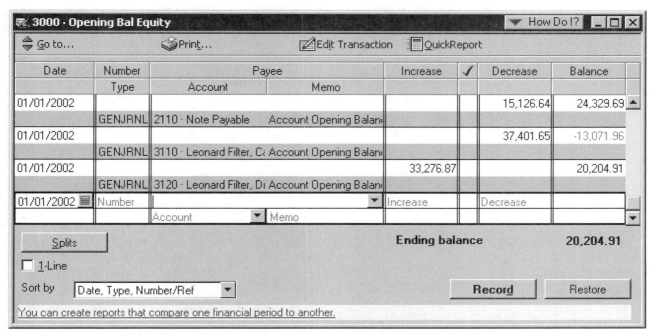

FIGURE 3.13 Opening Balance Equity Register

▶ If the account is an income account, key the balance into the Decrease column. If the account is an expense account, key the balance into the Increase column.

▶ Tab to the Account column and key the account number (the title will appear next to it).

▶ Click on Record.

STEP 26: From the Reports menu select the List option and then choose the Account Listing report and verify that you keyed the chart of accounts correctly.

STEP 27: From the Reports menu select the Accountant & Taxes option and then choose the Trial Balance report. Key a date range of January 1, 2002 to January 31, 2002 and verify that the account balances are correct. The Trial Balance report is shown in Figure 3.14 on the next page.

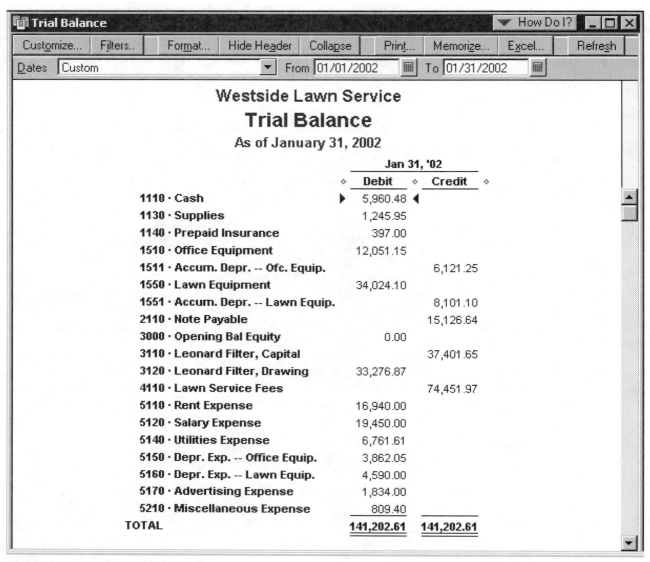

FIGURE 3.14 Trial Balance Report

SECTION 4

Demonstration Problem Solutions

04-D George Fielding, Consultant
Journal
December 2002

Date	Account	Debit	Credit
12/01/2002	101 · Cash	20,000.00	
	311 · George Fielding, Capital		20,000.00
		20,000.00	20,000.00
12/03/2002	521 · Rent Expense	1,000.00	
	101 · Cash		1,000.00
		1,000.00	1,000.00
12/04/2002	101 · Cash	2,500.00	
	401 · Professional Fees		2,500.00
		2,500.00	2,500.00
12/06/2002	533 · Utilities Expense	75.00	
	101 · Cash		75.00
		75.00	75.00
12/07/2002	101 · Cash	2,000.00	
	401 · Professional Fees		2,000.00
		2,000.00	2,000.00
12/12/2002	538 · Automobile Expense	60.00	
	101 · Cash		60.00
		60.00	60.00
12/14/2002	511 · Wages Expense	600.00	
	101 · Cash		600.00
		600.00	600.00
12/17/2002	142 · Office Supplies	280.00	
	202 · Accounts Payable		280.00
		280.00	280.00
12/20/2002	525 · Telephone Expense	100.00	
	101 · Cash		100.00
		100.00	100.00
12/21/2002	312 · George Fielding, Drawing	1,100.00	
	101 · Cash		1,100.00
		1,100.00	1,100.00
12/24/2002	534 · Charitable Contribution Expense	100.00	
	101 · Cash		100.00
		100.00	100.00
12/27/2002	101 · Cash	2,000.00	
	401 · Professional Fees		2,000.00
		2,000.00	2,000.00
12/28/2002	511 · Wages Expense	600.00	
	101 · Cash		600.00
		600.00	600.00
12/29/2002	202 · Accounts Payable	100.00	
	101 · Cash		100.00
		100.00	100.00
TOTAL		30,515.00	30,515.00

04-D George Fielding, Consultant
Trial Balance
As of December 31, 2002

	Dec 31, '02	
	Debit	Credit
101 · Cash	22,765.00	
142 · Office Supplies	280.00	
202 · Accounts Payable		180.00
311 · George Fielding, Capital		20,000.00
312 · George Fielding, Drawing	1,100.00	
401 · Professional Fees		6,500.00
511 · Wages Expense	1,200.00	
521 · Rent Expense	1,000.00	
525 · Telephone Expense	100.00	
533 · Utilities Expense	75.00	
534 · Charitable Contribution Expense	100.00	
538 · Automobile Expense	60.00	
TOTAL	26,680.00	26,680.00

05-D J. Park Legal Services
Trial Balance
As of December 31, 2002

	Dec 31, '02	
	Debit	Credit
101 · Cash	7,000.00	
142 · Office Supplies	800.00	
145 · Prepaid Insurance	1,200.00	
181 · Office Equipment	15,000.00	
187 · Computer Equipment	6,000.00	
201 · Notes Payable		5,000.00
202 · Accounts Payable		500.00
311 · Justin Park, Capital		11,400.00
312 · Justin Park, Drawing	5,000.00	
401 · Client Fees		40,000.00
511 · Wages Expense	12,000.00	
521 · Rent Expense	5,000.00	
525 · Telephone Expense	1,000.00	
533 · Utilities Expense	3,900.00	
TOTAL	56,900.00	56,900.00

05-D J. Park Legal Services
Journal
December 2002

Date	Memo	Account	Debit	Credit
12/31/2002	Adjusting Entry	523 · Office Supplies Expense	500.00	
	Adjusting Entry	142 · Office Supplies		500.00
			500.00	500.00
12/31/2002	Adjusting Entry	541 · Depr. Expense—Office Equip.	3,000.00	
	Adjusting Entry	181.1 · Accum. Depr.—Office Equipm...		3,000.00
			3,000.00	3,000.00
12/31/2002	Adjusting Entry	542 · Depr. Expense—Computer Equip.	1,000.00	
	Adjusting Entry	187.1 · Accum. Depr.—Computer Equ...		1,000.00
			1,000.00	1,000.00
12/31/2002	Adjusting Entry	535 · Insurance Expense	100.00	
	Adjusting Entry	145 · Prepaid Insurance		100.00
			100.00	100.00
12/31/2002	Adjusting Entry	511 · Wages Expense	300.00	
	Adjusting Entry	219 · Wages Payable		300.00
			300.00	300.00
TOTAL			4,900.00	4,900.00

05-D J. Park Legal Services
Profit & Loss
January through December 2002

	Jan - Dec '02
Income	
401 · Client Fees	40,000.00
Total Income	40,000.00
Expense	
511 · Wages Expense	12,300.00
521 · Rent Expense	5,000.00
523 · Office Supplies Expense	500.00
525 · Telephone Expense	1,000.00
533 · Utilities Expense	3,900.00
535 · Insurance Expense	100.00
541 · Depr. Expense--Office Equip.	3,000.00
542 · Depr. Expense--Computer Equip.	1,000.00
Total Expense	26,800.00
Net Income	13,200.00

05-D J. Park Legal Services
Balance Sheet
As of December 31, 2002

	Dec 31, '02
ASSETS	
Current Assets	
Checking/Savings	
101 · Cash	7,000.00
Total Checking/Savings	7,000.00
Other Current Assets	
142 · Office Supplies	300.00
145 · Prepaid Insurance	1,100.00
Total Other Current Assets	1,400.00
Total Current Assets	8,400.00
Fixed Assets	
181 · Office Equipment	15,000.00
181.1 · Accum. Depr.--Office Equipment	-3,000.00
187 · Computer Equipment	6,000.00
187.1 · Accum. Depr.--Computer Equip.	-1,000.00
Total Fixed Assets	17,000.00
TOTAL ASSETS	**25,400.00**
LIABILITIES & EQUITY	
Liabilities	
Current Liabilities	
Other Current Liabilities	
201 · Notes Payable	5,000.00
202 · Accounts Payable	500.00
219 · Wages Payable	300.00
Total Other Current Liabilities	5,800.00
Total Current Liabilities	5,800.00
Total Liabilities	5,800.00
Equity	
311 · Justin Park, Capital	11,400.00
312 · Justin Park, Drawing	-5,000.00
Net Income	13,200.00
Total Equity	19,600.00
TOTAL LIABILITIES & EQUITY	**25,400.00**

06-D Hard Copy Printers
Trial Balance
As of December 31, 2002

	Dec 31, '02	
	Debit	Credit
111 · Cash	1,180.00	
151 · Paper Supplies	3,600.00	
155 · Prepaid Insurance	1,000.00	
185 · Printing Equipment	5,800.00	
211 · Accounts Payable		500.00
311 · Timothy Chang, Capital		10,000.00
312 · Timothy Chang, Drawing	13,000.00	
411 · Printing Fees		35,100.00
541 · Wages Expense	11,970.00	
542 · Rent Expense	7,500.00	
544 · Telephone Expense	550.00	
545 · Utilities Expense	1,000.00	
TOTAL	45,600.00	45,600.00

06-D Hard Copy Printers
Journal
December 2002

Date	Memo	Account	Debit	Credit
12/31/2002	Adjusting Entry	543 · Paper Supplies Expense	3,550.00	
	Adjusting Entry	151 · Paper Supplies		3,550.00
			3,550.00	3,550.00
12/31/2002	Adjusting Entry	547 · Insurance Expense	505.00	
	Adjusting Entry	155 · Prepaid Insurance		505.00
			505.00	505.00
12/31/2002	Adjusting Entry	541 · Wages Expense	30.00	
	Adjusting Entry	219 · Wages Payable		30.00
			30.00	30.00
12/31/2002	Adjusting Entry	546 · Depr. Exp.–Printing Equipment	1,200.00	
	Adjusting Entry	185.1 · Accum. Depr.–Printing Equip.		1,200.00
			1,200.00	1,200.00
TOTAL			5,285.00	5,285.00

06-D Hard Copy Printers
Profit & Loss
January 2001 through December 2002

	Jan '01 - Dec '02
Income	
411 · Printing Fees	35,100.00
Total Income	35,100.00
Expense	
541 · Wages Expense	12,000.00
542 · Rent Expense	7,500.00
543 · Paper Supplies Expense	3,550.00
544 · Telephone Expense	550.00
545 · Utilities Expense	1,000.00
546 · Depr. Exp.—Printing Equipment	1,200.00
547 · Insurance Expense	505.00
Total Expense	26,305.00
Net Income	**8,795.00**

06-D Hard Copy Printers
Balance Sheet
As of December 31, 2002

	Dec 31, '02
ASSETS	
Current Assets	
Checking/Savings	
111 · Cash	1,180.00
Total Checking/Savings	1,180.00
Other Current Assets	
152 · Paper Supplies	50.00
155 · Prepaid Insurance	495.00
Total Other Current Assets	545.00
Total Current Assets	1,725.00
Fixed Assets	
185 · Printing Equipment	5,800.00
185,1 · Accum. Depr.--Printing Equip.	-1,200.00
Total Fixed Assets	4,600.00
TOTAL ASSETS	**6,325.00**
LIABILITIES & EQUITY	
Liabilities	
Current Liabilities	
Other Current Liabilities	
211 · Accounts Payable	500.00
219 · Wages Payable	30.00
Total Other Current Liabilities	530.00
Total Current Liabilities	530.00
Total Liabilities	530.00
Equity	
311 · Timothy Chang, Capital	10,000.00
312 · Timothy Chang, Drawing	-13,000.00
Net Income	8,795.00
Total Equity	5,795.00
TOTAL LIABILITIES & EQUITY	**6,325.00**

06-D Hard Copy Printers
Trial Balance
As of December 31, 2002

	Dec 31, '02	
	Debit	Credit
111 · Cash	1,180.00	
151 · Paper Supplies	50.00	
155 · Prepaid Insurance	495.00	
185 · Printing Equipment	5,800.00	
185.1 · Accum. Depr.--Printing Equip.		1,200.00
211 · Accounts Payable		500.00
219 · Wages Payable		30.00
311 · Timothy Chang, Capital		10,000.00
312 · Timothy Chang, Drawing	13,000.00	
411 · Printing Fees		35,100.00
541 · Wages Expense	12,000.00	
542 · Rent Expense	7,500.00	
543 · Paper Supplies Expense	3,550.00	
544 · Telephone Expense	550.00	
545 · Utilities Expense	1,000.00	
546 · Depr. Exp.--Printing Equipment	1,200.00	
547 · Insurance Expense	505.00	
TOTAL	46,830.00	46,830.00

06-D Hard Copy Printers
Trial Balance
As of January 1, 2003

	Jan 1, '03	
	Debit	Credit
111 · Cash	1,180.00	
152 · Paper Supplies	50.00	
155 · Prepaid Insurance	495.00	
185 · Printing Equipment	5,800.00	
185.1 · Accum. Depr.--Printing Equip.		1,200.00
211 · Accounts Payable		500.00
219 · Wages Payable		30.00
311 · Timothy Chang, Capital		5,795.00
TOTAL	7,525.00	7,525.00

Chapter 7 Demonstration Problem Solution

Reconciliation Report

03/03/2001

Cash account reconciled for the period ending 03/31/2002

Cleared Transactions

Previous Balance   6,051.62

Cleared Checks and Payments	12 Items	-1,479.80
Cleared Deposits and Other Credits	1 Items	847.18

Cleared Balance   5,419.00

Uncleared Transactions

Uncleared Checks and Payments	5 Items	-1,830.08
Uncleared Deposits and Other Credits	1 Items	926.10

New Transactions

Account Balance as of 03/31/2002 (statement closing date)   4,515.02

New Checks and Payments	0 Items	0.00
New Deposits and Other Credits	0 Items	0.00

Ending Account Balance   4,515.02

07-D Kuhn's Wilderness Outfitters
Custom Transaction Detail Report
March 31, 2002

Date	Num	Name	Account	Debit	Credit
Mar 31, '02					
03/31/2002	477		101 · Cash		197.45
03/31/2002	477		534 · Automobile Expense	32.40	
03/31/2002	477		536 · Postage Expense	27.50	
03/31/2002	477		537 · Charitable Contributions Exp.	35.00	
03/31/2002	477		525 · Telephone Expense	6.20	
03/31/2002	477		538 · Travel & Entertainment Exp.	38.60	
03/31/2002	477		610 · Miscellaneous Expense	17.75	
03/31/2002	477		312 · Jason Kuhn, Drawing	40.00	
03/31/2002			101 · Cash		154.00
03/31/2002		Office Suppliers, Inc.	202 · Accounts Payable	54.00	
03/31/2002			312 · Jason Kuhn, Drawing	100.00	
03/31/2002			101 · Cash		4.10
03/31/2002			610 · Miscellaneous Expense	4.10	
Mar 31, '02				**355.55**	**355.55**

08-D Canine Coiffures
Payroll Summary
January 15 - 23, 2002

	John Shapiro			Katie DeNourie
	Hours	Rate	Jan 15 - 23, '02	Hours
Employee Wages, Taxes and Adjustments				
Gross Pay				
Hourly Regular Rate	40	11.50	460.00	40
Overtime Hourly Rate		17.25	0.00	4
Total Gross Pay			460.00	
Deductions from Gross Pay				
Credit Union			-15.00	
Health Insurance			0.00	
Savings Bonds			-18.75	
Total Deductions from Gross Pay			-33.75	
Adjusted Gross Pay			426.25	
Taxes Withheld				
Federal Withholding			-44.00	
Medicare Employee			-6.67	
Social Security Employee			-28.52	
City Tax			-4.60	
Total Taxes Withheld			-83.79	
Net Pay			**342.46**	
Employer Taxes and Contributions				
Federal Unemployment			0.00	
Medicare Company			6.67	
Social Security Company			28.52	
Total Employer Taxes and Contributions			**35.19**	

Page 1

Payroll Summary
January 15 - 23, 2002

	Katie DeNourie		Nancy Parker	
	Rate	Jan 15 - 23, '02	Hours	Rate
Employee Wages, Taxes and Adjustments				
Gross Pay				
Hourly Regular Rate	11.50	460.00	40	11.00
Overtime Hourly Rate	17.25	69.00	2	16.50
Total Gross Pay		529.00		
Deductions from Gross Pay				
Credit Union		-15.00		
Health Insurance		-4.00		
Savings Bonds		0.00		
Total Deductions from Gross Pay		-19.00		
Adjusted Gross Pay		510.00		
Taxes Withheld				
Federal Withholding		-55.00		
Medicare Employee		-7.67		
Social Security Employee		-32.80		
City Tax		-5.29		
Total Taxes Withheld		-100.76		
Net Pay		409.24		
Employer Taxes and Contributions				
Federal Unemployment		0.00		
Medicare Company		7.67		
Social Security Company		32.80		
Total Employer Taxes and Contributions		40.47		

Page 2

08-D Canine Coiffures
Payroll Summary
January 15 - 23, 2002

	Nancy Parker	Pete Garriott		
	Jan 15 - 23, '02	Hours	Rate	Jan 15 - 23, '02
Employee Wages, Taxes and Adjustments				
Gross Pay				
Hourly Regular Rate	440.00	40	12.00	480.00
Overtime Hourly Rate	33.00		18.00	0.00
Total Gross Pay	473.00			480.00
Deductions from Gross Pay				
Credit Union	0.00			0.00
Health Insurance	-14.00			-14.00
Savings Bonds	0.00			-18.75
Total Deductions from Gross Pay	-14.00			-32.75
Adjusted Gross Pay	459.00			447.25
Taxes Withheld				
Federal Withholding	-20.00			-46.00
Medicare Employee	-6.86			-6.96
Social Security Employee	-29.33			-29.76
City Tax	-4.73			-4.80
Total Taxes Withheld	-60.92			-87.52
Net Pay	398.08			359.73
Employer Taxes and Contributions				
Federal Unemployment	0.00			0.00
Medicare Company	6.86			6.96
Social Security Company	29.33			29.76
Total Employer Taxes and Contributions	36.19			36.72

Page 3

08-D Canine Coiffures
Payroll Summary
January 15 - 23, 2002

	Sheila Martinez			TOTAL
	Hours	Rate	Jan 15 - 23, '02	Hours
Employee Wages, Taxes and Adjustments				
Gross Pay				
Hourly Regular Rate	39	12.50	487.50	199.00
Overtime Hourly Rate		18.75	0.00	6.00
Total Gross Pay			487.50	
Deductions from Gross Pay				
Credit Union			-15.00	
Health Insurance			-4.00	
Savings Bonds			0.00	
Total Deductions from Gross Pay			-19.00	
Adjusted Gross Pay			468.50	
Taxes Withheld				
Federal Withholding			-30.00	
Medicare Employee			-7.07	
Social Security Employee			-30.23	
City Tax			-4.88	
Total Taxes Withheld			-72.18	
Net Pay			396.32	
Employer Taxes and Contributions				
Federal Unemployment			0.00	
Medicare Company			7.07	
Social Security Company			30.23	
Total Employer Taxes and Contributions			**37.30**	

08-D Canine Coiffures
Payroll Summary
January 15 - 23, 2002

	TOTAL	
	Rate	Jan 15 - 23, '02
Employee Wages, Taxes and Adjustments		
Gross Pay		
Hourly Regular Rate		2,327.50
Overtime Hourly Rate		102.00
Total Gross Pay		2,429.50
Deductions from Gross Pay		
Credit Union		-45.00
Health Insurance		-36.00
Savings Bonds		-37.50
Total Deductions from Gross Pay		-118.50
Adjusted Gross Pay		2,311.00
Taxes Withheld		
Federal Withholding		-195.00
Medicare Employee		-35.23
Social Security Employee		-150.64
City Tax		-24.30
Total Taxes Withheld		-405.17
Net Pay		**1,905.83**
Employer Taxes and Contributions		
Federal Unemployment		0.00
Medicare Company		35.23
Social Security Company		150.64
Total Employer Taxes and Contributions		**185.87**

08-D Canine Coiffures
Payroll Liabilities
January 15 - 23, 2002

	Jan 15 - 23, '02
Payroll Liabilities	
Federal Withholding	195.00
Medicare Employee	35.23
Social Security Employee	150.64
Federal Unemployment	0.00
Medicare Company	35.23
Social Security Company	150.64
City Tax	24.30
Credit Union	45.00
Health Insurance	36.00
Savings Bonds	37.50
Total Payroll Liabilities	**709.54**

Journal
January 15 - 23, 2002

Type	Date	Name	Account	Debit	Credit
Paycheck	01/23/2002	John Shapiro	101 · Cash		342.46
		John Shapiro	511 · Wages and Salaries Expense	460.00	
		John Shapiro	511 · Wages and Salaries Expense	0.00	
		John Shapiro	217 · Credit Union Payable		15.00
		John Shapiro	218 · Savings Bond Deduct. Payable		18.75
		John Shapiro	2100 · Payroll Liabilities		44.00
		John Shapiro	511 · Wages and Salaries Expense	28.52	
		John Shapiro	2100 · Payroll Liabilities		28.52
		John Shapiro	2100 · Payroll Liabilities		28.52
		John Shapiro	511 · Wages and Salaries Expense	6.67	
		John Shapiro	2100 · Payroll Liabilities		6.67
		John Shapiro	2100 · Payroll Liabilities		6.67
		John Shapiro	511 · Wages and Salaries Expense	0.00	
		John Shapiro	2100 · Payroll Liabilities	0.00	
		John Shapiro	215 · City Earnings Payable		4.60
				495.19	495.19
Paycheck	01/23/2002	Katie DeNourie	101 · Cash		409.24
		Katie DeNourie	511 · Wages and Salaries Expense	460.00	
		Katie DeNourie	511 · Wages and Salaries Expense	69.00	
		Katie DeNourie	216 · Health Insurance Prem Payable		4.00
		Katie DeNourie	217 · Credit Union Payable		15.00
		Katie DeNourie	2100 · Payroll Liabilities		55.00
		Katie DeNourie	511 · Wages and Salaries Expense	32.80	
		Katie DeNourie	2100 · Payroll Liabilities		32.80
		Katie DeNourie	2100 · Payroll Liabilities		32.80
		Katie DeNourie	511 · Wages and Salaries Expense	7.67	
		Katie DeNourie	2100 · Payroll Liabilities		7.67
		Katie DeNourie	2100 · Payroll Liabilities		7.67
		Katie DeNourie	511 · Wages and Salaries Expense	0.00	
		Katie DeNourie	2100 · Payroll Liabilities	0.00	
		Katie DeNourie	215 · City Earnings Payable		5.29
				569.47	569.47
Paycheck	01/23/2002	Nancy Parker	101 · Cash		398.08
		Nancy Parker	511 · Wages and Salaries Expense	440.00	
		Nancy Parker	511 · Wages and Salaries Expense	33.00	
		Nancy Parker	216 · Health Insurance Prem Payable		14.00
		Nancy Parker	2100 · Payroll Liabilities		20.00
		Nancy Parker	511 · Wages and Salaries Expense	29.33	
		Nancy Parker	2100 · Payroll Liabilities		29.33
		Nancy Parker	2100 · Payroll Liabilities		29.33
		Nancy Parker	511 · Wages and Salaries Expense	6.86	
		Nancy Parker	2100 · Payroll Liabilities		6.86
		Nancy Parker	2100 · Payroll Liabilities		6.86
		Nancy Parker	511 · Wages and Salaries Expense	0.00	
		Nancy Parker	2100 · Payroll Liabilities	0.00	
		Nancy Parker	215 · City Earnings Payable		4.73
				509.19	509.19
Paycheck	01/23/2002	Pete Garriott	101 · Cash		359.73
		Pete Garriott	511 · Wages and Salaries Expense	480.00	
		Pete Garriott	511 · Wages and Salaries Expense	0.00	
		Pete Garriott	216 · Health Insurance Prem Payable		14.00
		Pete Garriott	218 · Savings Bond Deduct. Payable		18.75
		Pete Garriott	2100 · Payroll Liabilities		46.00
		Pete Garriott	511 · Wages and Salaries Expense	29.76	
		Pete Garriott	2100 · Payroll Liabilities		29.76
		Pete Garriott	2100 · Payroll Liabilities		29.76
		Pete Garriott	511 · Wages and Salaries Expense	6.96	
		Pete Garriott	2100 · Payroll Liabilities		6.96
		Pete Garriott	2100 · Payroll Liabilities		6.96
		Pete Garriott	511 · Wages and Salaries Expense	0.00	

08-D Canine Coiffures
Journal
January 15 - 23, 2002

Type	Date	Name	Account	Debit	Credit
		Pete Garriott	2100 · Payroll Liabilities	0.00	
		Pete Garriott	215 · City Earnings Payable		4.80
				516.72	516.72
Paycheck	01/23/2002	Sheila Martinez	101 · Cash		396.32
		Sheila Martinez	511 · Wages and Salaries Expense	487.50	
		Sheila Martinez	511 · Wages and Salaries Expense	0.00	
		Sheila Martinez	216 · Health Insurance Prem Payable		4.00
		Sheila Martinez	217 · Credit Union Payable		15.00
		Sheila Martinez	2100 · Payroll Liabilities		30.00
		Sheila Martinez	511 · Wages and Salaries Expense	30.23	
		Sheila Martinez	2100 · Payroll Liabilities		30.23
		Sheila Martinez	2100 · Payroll Liabilities		30.23
		Sheila Martinez	511 · Wages and Salaries Expense	7.07	
		Sheila Martinez	2100 · Payroll Liabilities		7.07
		Sheila Martinez	2100 · Payroll Liabilities		7.07
		Sheila Martinez	511 · Wages and Salaries Expense	0.00	
		Sheila Martinez	2100 · Payroll Liabilities	0.00	
		Sheila Martinez	215 · City Earnings Payable		4.88
				524.80	524.80
TOTAL				**2,615.37**	**2,615.37**

Page 2

— 127 —

09-D Hart Company
Journal
December 2002

Date	Account	Debit	Credit
12/31/2002	511 · Wages and Salaries Expense	3,800.00	
	211 · Employee Income Tax Payable		380.00
	212 · Social Security Tax Payable		235.60
	213 · Medicare Tax Payable		55.10
	216 · Health Insurance Premiums Pay.		50.00
	217 · United Way Contributions Pay.		100.00
	101 · Cash		2,979.30
		3,800.00	3,800.00
12/31/2002	513 · Payroll Taxes Expense	315.50	
	212 · Social Security Tax Payable		235.60
	213 · Medicare Tax Payable		55.10
	219 · FUTA Tax Payable		3.20
	220 · SUTA Tax Payable		21.60
		315.50	315.50
TOTAL		**4,115.50**	**4,115.50**

09-D Hart Company
Journal
January 2003

Date	Account	Debit	Credit
01/15/2003	211 · Employee Income Tax Payable	1,520.00	
	212 · Social Security Tax Payable	1,847.00	
	213 · Medicare Tax Payable	433.00	
	101 · Cash		3,800.00
		3,800.00	3,800.00
01/31/2003	219 · FUTA Tax Payable	27.20	
	101 · Cash		27.20
		27.20	27.20
01/31/2003	220 · SUTA Tax Payable	183.60	
	101 · Cash		183.60
		183.60	183.60
01/31/2003	510 · Workers Compensation Ins. Exp.	18.00	
	221 · Workers' Compensation Ins. Pay.		18.00
		18.00	18.00
TOTAL		**4,028.80**	**4,028.80**

10-D Vietor Financial Planning
Journal
December 2002

Date	Name	Account	Debit	Credit
12/01/2002		101 · Cash	20,000.00	
		311 · Maria Vietor, Capital		20,000.00
			20,000.00	20,000.00
12/03/2002		521 · Rent Expense	1,000.00	
		101 · Cash		1,000.00
			1,000.00	1,000.00
12/04/2002		101 · Cash	2,500.00	
		401 · Professional Fees		2,500.00
			2,500.00	2,500.00
12/06/2002		533 · Utilities Expense	75.00	
		101 · Cash		75.00
			75.00	75.00
12/07/2002		101 · Cash	2,000.00	
		401 · Professional Fees		2,000.00
			2,000.00	2,000.00
12/12/2002		526 · Automobile Expense	60.00	
		101 · Cash		60.00
			60.00	60.00
12/14/2002		511 · Wages Expense	600.00	
		101 · Cash		600.00
			600.00	600.00
12/17/2002		142 · Office Supplies	280.00	
	Cleat Office Supply	202 · Accounts Payable		280.00
			280.00	280.00
12/20/2002		525 · Telephone Expense	100.00	
		101 · Cash		100.00
			100.00	100.00
12/21/2002		312 · Maria Vietor, Drawing	1,100.00	
		101 · Cash		1,100.00
			1,100.00	1,100.00
12/24/2002		534 · Charitable Contributions Exp.	100.00	
		101 · Cash		100.00
			100.00	100.00
12/27/2002		101 · Cash	2,000.00	
		401 · Professional Fees		2,000.00
			2,000.00	2,000.00
12/28/2002		511 · Wages Expense	600.00	
		101 · Cash		600.00
			600.00	600.00
12/29/2002	Cleat Office Supply	202 · Accounts Payable	100.00	
	Cleat Office Supply	101 · Cash		100.00
			100.00	100.00
TOTAL			30,515.00	30,515.00

10-D Vietor Financial Planning
General Ledger
As of December 31, 2002

Type	Date	Name	Debit	Credit	Balance
101 · Cash					0.00
General Journal	12/01/2002		20,000.00		20,000.00
General Journal	12/03/2002			1,000.00	19,000.00
General Journal	12/04/2002		2,500.00		21,500.00
General Journal	12/06/2002			75.00	21,425.00
General Journal	12/07/2002		2,000.00		23,425.00
General Journal	12/12/2002			60.00	23,365.00
General Journal	12/14/2002			600.00	22,765.00
General Journal	12/20/2002			100.00	22,665.00
General Journal	12/21/2002			1,100.00	21,565.00
General Journal	12/24/2002			100.00	21,465.00
General Journal	12/27/2002		2,000.00		23,465.00
General Journal	12/28/2002			600.00	22,865.00
General Journal	12/29/2002	Cleat Office Supply		100.00	22,765.00
Total 101 · Cash			26,500.00	3,735.00	22,765.00
142 · Office Supplies					0.00
General Journal	12/17/2002		280.00		280.00
Total 142 · Office Supplies			280.00	0.00	280.00
202 · Accounts Payable					0.00
General Journal	12/17/2002	Cleat Office Supply		280.00	-280.00
General Journal	12/29/2002	Cleat Office Supply	100.00		-180.00
Total 202 · Accounts Payable			100.00	280.00	-180.00
311 · Maria Vietor, Capital					0.00
General Journal	12/01/2002			20,000.00	-20,000.00
Total 311 · Maria Vietor, Capital			0.00	20,000.00	-20,000.00
312 · Maria Vietor, Drawing					0.00
General Journal	12/21/2002		1,100.00		1,100.00
Total 312 · Maria Vietor, Drawing			1,100.00	0.00	1,100.00
401 · Professional Fees					0.00
General Journal	12/04/2002			2,500.00	-2,500.00
General Journal	12/07/2002			2,000.00	-4,500.00
General Journal	12/27/2002			2,000.00	-6,500.00
Total 401 · Professional Fees			0.00	6,500.00	-6,500.00
511 · Wages Expense					0.00
General Journal	12/14/2002		600.00		600.00
General Journal	12/28/2002		600.00		1,200.00
Total 511 · Wages Expense			1,200.00	0.00	1,200.00
521 · Rent Expense					0.00
General Journal	12/03/2002		1,000.00		1,000.00
Total 521 · Rent Expense			1,000.00	0.00	1,000.00
525 · Telephone Expense					0.00
General Journal	12/20/2002		100.00		100.00
Total 525 · Telephone Expense			100.00	0.00	100.00
526 · Automobile Expense					0.00
General Journal	12/12/2002		60.00		60.00
Total 526 · Automobile Expense			60.00	0.00	60.00
533 · Utilities Expense					0.00
General Journal	12/06/2002		75.00		75.00
Total 533 · Utilities Expense			75.00	0.00	75.00
534 · Charitable Contributions Exp.					0.00
General Journal	12/24/2002		100.00		100.00
Total 534 · Charitable Contributions Exp.			100.00	0.00	100.00
TOTAL			**30,515.00**	**30,515.00**	**0.00**

Page 1

— 130 —

10-D Vietor Financial Planning
Trial Balance
As of December 31, 2002

| | Dec 31, '02 | |
	Debit	Credit
101 · Cash	22,765.00	
142 · Office Supplies	280.00	
202 · Accounts Payable		180.00
311 · Maria Vietor, Capital		20,000.00
312 · Maria Vietor, Drawing	1,100.00	
401 · Professional Fees		6,500.00
511 · Wages Expense	1,200.00	
521 · Rent Expense	1,000.00	
525 · Telephone Expense	100.00	
526 · Automobile Expense	60.00	
533 · Utilities Expense	75.00	
534 · Charitable Contributions Exp.	100.00	
TOTAL	**26,680.00**	**26,680.00**

11-D Hunt's Audio-Video Store
Journal
April 2002

Date	Num	Name	Account	Debit	Credit
04/03/2002	S41	Susan Haberman	122 · Accounts Receivable	170.67	
		Susan Haberman	401 · Sales		159.50
		Susan Haberman	231 · Sales Tax Payable		11.17
				170.67	170.67
04/04/2002	S42	Goro Kimura	122 · Accounts Receivable	320.95	
		Goro Kimura	401 · Sales		299.95
		Goro Kimura	231 · Sales Tax Payable		21.00
				320.95	320.95
04/06/2002			101 · Cash	69.50	
		Tera Scherrer	122 · Accounts Receivable		69.50
				69.50	69.50
04/07/2002			401.1 · Sales Returns and Allowa...	39.95	
			231 · Sales Tax Payable	2.80	
		Kenneth Watt	122 · Accounts Receivable		42.75
				42.75	42.75
04/10/2002			101 · Cash	99.95	
		Kelllie Cokley	122 · Accounts Receivable		99.95
				99.95	99.95
04/11/2002	S43	Victor Cardona	122 · Accounts Receivable	534.95	
		Victor Cardona	401 · Sales		499.95
		Victor Cardona	231 · Sales Tax Payable		35.00
				534.95	534.95
04/14/2002			101 · Cash	157.00	
		Kenneth Watt	122 · Accounts Receivable		157.00
				157.00	157.00
04/17/2002	S44	Susan Haberman	122 · Accounts Receivable	406.55	
		Susan Haberman	401 · Sales		379.95
		Susan Haberman	231 · Sales Tax Payable		26.60
				406.55	406.55
04/19/2002	S45	Tera Scherrer	122 · Accounts Receivable	64.15	
		Tera Scherrer	401 · Sales		59.95
		Tera Scherrer	231 · Sales Tax Payable		4.20
				64.15	64.15
04/21/2002			401.1 · Sales Returns and Allowa...	49.95	
			231 · Sales Tax Payable	3.50	
		Goro Kimura	122 · Accounts Receivable		53.45
				53.45	53.45
04/24/2002			101 · Cash	299.95	
		Victor Cardona	122 · Accounts Receivable		299.95
				299.95	299.95
04/25/2002	S46	Kelllie Cokley	122 · Accounts Receivable	192.07	
		Kelllie Cokley	401 · Sales		179.50
		Kelllie Cokley	231 · Sales Tax Payable		12.57
				192.07	192.07
04/26/2002			101 · Cash	250.65	
		Susan Haberman	122 · Accounts Receivable		250.65
				250.65	250.65
04/28/2002	S47	Kenneth Watt	122 · Accounts Receivable	53.45	
		Kenneth Watt	401 · Sales		49.95
		Kenneth Watt	231 · Sales Tax Payable		3.50

Page 1

11-D Hunt's Audio-Video Store
Journal
April 2002

Date	Num	Name	Account	Debit	Credit
				53.45	53.45
04/30/2002			101 · Cash	1,240.13	
			513 · Bank Credit Card Expense	65.27	
			401 · Sales		1,220.00
			231 · Sales Tax Payable		85.40
				1,305.40	1,305.40
04/30/2002			101 · Cash	2,140.00	
			401 · Sales		2,000.00
			231 · Sales Tax Payable		140.00
				2,140.00	2,140.00
TOTAL				**6,161.44**	**6,161.44**

11-D Hunt's Audio-Video Store
General Ledger
As of April 30, 2002

Type	Date	Name	Debit	Credit	Balance
101 · Cash					5,000.00
General Journal	04/06/2002		69.50		5,069.50
General Journal	04/10/2002		99.95		5,169.45
General Journal	04/14/2002		157.00		5,326.45
General Journal	04/24/2002		299.95		5,626.40
General Journal	04/26/2002		250.65		5,877.05
General Journal	04/30/2002		1,240.13		7,117.18
General Journal	04/30/2002		2,140.00		9,257.18
Total 101 · Cash			4,257.18	0.00	9,257.18
122 · Accounts Receivable					1,208.63
General Journal	04/03/2002	Susan Haberman	170.67		1,379.30
General Journal	04/04/2002	Goro Kimura	320.95		1,700.25
General Journal	04/06/2002	Tera Scherrer		69.50	1,630.75
General Journal	04/07/2002	Kenneth Watt		42.75	1,588.00
General Journal	04/10/2002	Kelllie Cokley		99.95	1,488.05
General Journal	04/11/2002	Victor Cardona	534.95		2,023.00
General Journal	04/14/2002	Kenneth Watt		157.00	1,866.00
General Journal	04/17/2002	Susan Haberman	406.55		2,272.55
General Journal	04/19/2002	Tera Scherrer	64.15		2,336.70
General Journal	04/21/2002	Goro Kimura		53.45	2,283.25
General Journal	04/24/2002	Victor Cardona		299.95	1,983.30
General Journal	04/25/2002	Kelllie Cokley	192.07		2,175.37
General Journal	04/26/2002	Susan Haberman		250.65	1,924.72
General Journal	04/28/2002	Kenneth Watt	53.45		1,978.17
Total 122 · Accounts Receivable			1,742.79	973.25	1,978.17
141 · Merchandise Inventory					31,260.08
Total 141 · Merchandise Inventory					31,260.08
231 · Sales Tax Payable					-72.52
General Journal	04/03/2002	Susan Haberman		11.17	-83.69
General Journal	04/04/2002	Goro Kimura		21.00	-104.69
General Journal	04/07/2002		2.80		-101.89
General Journal	04/11/2002	Victor Cardona		35.00	-136.89
General Journal	04/17/2002	Susan Haberman		26.60	-163.49
General Journal	04/19/2002	Tera Scherrer		4.20	-167.69
General Journal	04/21/2002		3.50		-164.19
General Journal	04/25/2002	Kelllie Cokley		12.57	-176.76
General Journal	04/28/2002	Kenneth Watt		3.50	-180.26
General Journal	04/30/2002			85.40	-265.66
General Journal	04/30/2002			140.00	-405.66
Total 231 · Sales Tax Payable			6.30	339.44	-405.66
311 · Karen Hunt, Capital					-40,000.00
Total 311 · Karen Hunt, Capital					-40,000.00
401 · Sales					-8,421.49
General Journal	04/03/2002	Susan Haberman		159.50	-8,580.99
General Journal	04/04/2002	Goro Kimura		299.95	-8,880.94
General Journal	04/11/2002	Victor Cardona		499.95	-9,380.89
General Journal	04/17/2002	Susan Haberman		379.95	-9,760.84
General Journal	04/19/2002	Tera Scherrer		59.95	-9,820.79
General Journal	04/25/2002	Kelllie Cokley		179.50	-10,000.29
General Journal	04/28/2002	Kenneth Watt		49.95	-10,050.24
General Journal	04/30/2002			1,220.00	-11,270.24
General Journal	04/30/2002			2,000.00	-13,270.24
Total 401 · Sales			0.00	4,848.75	-13,270.24
401.1 · Sales Returns and Allowances					168.43
General Journal	04/07/2002		39.95		208.38
General Journal	04/21/2002		49.95		258.33
Total 401.1 · Sales Returns and Allowances			89.90	0.00	258.33

Page 1

— 134 —

11-D Hunt's Audio-Video Store
General Ledger
As of April 30, 2002

Type	Date	Name	Debit	Credit	Balance
501 · Purchases					10,641.87
Total 501 · Purchases					10,641.87
513 · Bank Credit Card Expense					215.00
General Journal	04/30/2002		65.27		280.27
Total 513 · Bank Credit Card Expense			65.27	0.00	280.27
TOTAL			**6,161.44**	**6,161.44**	**0.00**

11-D Hunt's Audio-Video Store
Customer Balance Summary
As of April 30, 2002

	Apr 30, '02
Goro Kimura	647.00
Kellie Cokley	192.07
Kenneth Watt	53.45
Susan Haberman	406.55
Tera Scherrer	144.15
Victor Cardona	534.95
TOTAL	**1,978.17**

12-D Rutman Pharmacy
Journal
June 2002

Date	Num	Name	Account	Debit	Credit
06/01/2002	71		501 · Purchases	234.20	
		Sullivan Co.	202 · Accounts Payable		234.20
				234.20	234.20
06/02/2002	CK536		521 · Rent Expense	1,000.00	
			101 · Cash		1,000.00
				1,000.00	1,000.00
06/05/2002	196		501 · Purchases	562.40	
		Amfac Drug Supply	202 · Accounts Payable		562.40
				562.40	562.40
06/07/2002	914A		501 · Purchases	367.35	
		University Drug Co.	202 · Accounts Payable		367.35
				367.35	367.35
06/09/2002	CK537	Sullivan Co.	202 · Accounts Payable	234.20	
		Sullivan Co.	101 · Cash		229.52
		Sullivan Co.	501.2 · Purchases Discounts		4.68
				234.20	234.20
06/12/2002		Amfac Drug Supply	202 · Accounts Payable	46.20	
		Amfac Drug Supply	501.1 · Purchases Returns & Allowan...		46.20
				46.20	46.20
06/14/2002	745		501 · Purchases	479.40	
		Mutual Drug Co.	202 · Accounts Payable		479.40
				479.40	479.40
06/15/2002		University Drug Co.	202 · Accounts Payable	53.70	
		University Drug Co.	501.1 · Purchases Returns & Allowan...		53.70
				53.70	53.70
06/16/2002	CK538	Amfac Drug Supply	202 · Accounts Payable	516.20	
		Amfac Drug Supply	101 · Cash		511.04
		Amfac Drug Supply	501.2 · Purchases Discounts		5.16
				516.20	516.20
06/23/2002	CK539	Mutual Drug Co.	202 · Accounts Payable	479.40	
		Mutual Drug Co.	101 · Cash		469.81
		Mutual Drug Co.	501.2 · Purchases Discounts		9.59
				479.40	479.40
06/27/2002	675		501 · Purchases	638.47	
		Flites Pharmaceuticals	202 · Accounts Payable		638.47
				638.47	638.47
06/29/2002	CK540		501 · Purchases	270.20	
			101 · Cash		270.20
				270.20	270.20
06/30/2002	CK541	Vashon Medical Supply	202 · Accounts Payable	1,217.69	
		Vashon Medical Supply	101 · Cash		1,217.69
				1,217.69	1,217.69
TOTAL				**6,099.41**	**6,099.41**

Page 1

12-D Rutman Pharmacy
General Ledger
As of June 30, 2002

Type	Date	Name	Debit	Credit	Balance
101 · Cash					9,180.00
General Journal	06/02/2002			1,000.00	8,180.00
General Journal	06/09/2002	Sullivan Co.		229.52	7,950.48
General Journal	06/16/2002	Amfac Drug Supply		511.04	7,439.44
General Journal	06/23/2002	Mutual Drug Co.		469.81	6,969.63
General Journal	06/29/2002			270.20	6,699.43
General Journal	06/30/2002	Vashon Medical Supply		1,217.69	5,481.74
Total 101 · Cash			0.00	3,698.26	5,481.74
141 · Merchandise Inventory					24,700.00
Total 141 · Merchandise Inventory					24,700.00
202 · Accounts Payable					-1,217.69
General Journal	06/01/2002	Sullivan Co.		234.20	-1,451.89
General Journal	06/05/2002	Amfac Drug Supply		562.40	-2,014.29
General Journal	06/07/2002	University Drug Co.		367.35	-2,381.64
General Journal	06/09/2002	Sullivan Co.	234.20		-2,147.44
General Journal	06/12/2002	Amfac Drug Supply	46.20		-2,101.24
General Journal	06/14/2002	Mutual Drug Co.		479.40	-2,580.64
General Journal	06/15/2002	University Drug Co.	53.70		-2,526.94
General Journal	06/16/2002	Amfac Drug Supply	516.20		-2,010.74
General Journal	06/23/2002	Mutual Drug Co.	479.40		-1,531.34
General Journal	06/27/2002	Flites Pharmaceuticals		638.47	-2,169.81
General Journal	06/30/2002	Vashon Medical Supply	1,217.69		-952.12
Total 202 · Accounts Payable			2,547.39	2,281.82	-952.12
311 · Jodi Rutman, Capital					-20,023.23
Total 311 · Jodi Rutman, Capital					-20,023.23
411 · Sales					-30,941.25
Total 411 · Sales					-30,941.25
501 · Purchases					13,826.25
General Journal	06/01/2002		234.20		14,060.45
General Journal	06/05/2002		562.40		14,622.85
General Journal	06/07/2002		367.35		14,990.20
General Journal	06/14/2002		479.40		15,469.60
General Journal	06/27/2002		638.47		16,108.07
General Journal	06/29/2002		270.20		16,378.27
Total 501 · Purchases			2,552.02	0.00	16,378.27
501.1 · Purchases Returns & Allowances					-312.63
General Journal	06/12/2002	Amfac Drug Supply		46.20	-358.83
General Journal	06/15/2002	University Drug Co.		53.70	-412.53
Total 501.1 · Purchases Returns & Allowances			0.00	99.90	-412.53
501.2 · Purchases Discounts					-211.45
General Journal	06/09/2002	Sullivan Co.		4.68	-216.13
General Journal	06/16/2002	Amfac Drug Supply		5.16	-221.29
General Journal	06/23/2002	Mutual Drug Co.		9.59	-230.88
Total 501.2 · Purchases Discounts			0.00	19.43	-230.88
521 · Rent Expense					5,000.00
General Journal	06/02/2002		1,000.00		6,000.00
Total 521 · Rent Expense			1,000.00	0.00	6,000.00
TOTAL			6,099.41	6,099.41	0.00

12-D Rutman Pharmacy
Vendor Balance Summary
As of June 30, 2002

	Jun 30, '02
Flites Pharmaceuticals	638.47
University Drug Co.	313.65
TOTAL	**952.12**

12-D Rutman Pharmacy
Vendor Balance Detail
As of June 30, 2002

Type	Date	Num	Account	Amount	Balance
Amfac Drug Supply					0.00
General Journal	06/05/2002	196	202 · Accounts Payable	562.40	562.40
General Journal	06/12/2002		202 · Accounts Payable	-46.20	516.20
General Journal	06/16/2002	CK538	202 · Accounts Payable	-516.20	0.00
Total Amfac Drug Supply				0.00	0.00
Flites Pharmaceuticals					0.00
General Journal	06/27/2002	675	202 · Accounts Payable	638.47	638.47
Total Flites Pharmaceuticals				638.47	638.47
Mutual Drug Co.					0.00
General Journal	06/14/2002	745	202 · Accounts Payable	479.40	479.40
General Journal	06/23/2002	CK539	202 · Accounts Payable	-479.40	0.00
Total Mutual Drug Co.				0.00	0.00
Sullivan Co.					0.00
General Journal	06/01/2002	71	202 · Accounts Payable	234.20	234.20
General Journal	06/09/2002	CK537	202 · Accounts Payable	-234.20	0.00
Total Sullivan Co.				0.00	0.00
University Drug Co.					0.00
General Journal	06/07/2002	914A	202 · Accounts Payable	367.35	367.35
General Journal	06/15/2002		202 · Accounts Payable	-53.70	313.65
Total University Drug Co.				313.65	313.65
Vashon Medical Supply					1,217.69
General Journal	06/30/2002	CK541	202 · Accounts Payable	-1,217.69	0.00
Total Vashon Medical Supply				-1,217.69	0.00
TOTAL				**-265.57**	**952.12**

13-D David's Specialty Shop
Journal
May 2002

Date	Num	Name	Account	Debit	Credit
05/01/2002	533	Molly Mac	122 · Accounts Receivable	2,100.00	
		Molly Mac	401 · Sales		2,000.00
		Molly Mac	231 · Sales Tax Payable		100.00
				2,100.00	2,100.00
05/02/2002	750	Kari Co.	202 · Accounts Payable	800.00	
		Kari Co.	101 · Cash		784.00
		Kari Co.	501.2 · Purchases Discounts		16.00
				800.00	800.00
05/03/2002	621		501 · Purchases	2,000.00	
		Scanlan Wholesalers	202 · Accounts Payable		2,000.00
				2,000.00	2,000.00
05/04/2002	767		501 · Purchases	1,500.00	
		Simpson Enterprises	202 · Accounts Payable		1,500.00
				1,500.00	1,500.00
05/04/2002	751		545 · Telephone Expense	200.00	
			101 · Cash		200.00
				200.00	200.00
05/08/2002			101 · Cash	3,780.00	
			401 · Sales		3,600.00
			231 · Sales Tax Payable		180.00
				3,780.00	3,780.00
05/09/2002			101 · Cash	2,500.00	
		Cody Slaton	122 · Accounts Receivable		2,500.00
				2,500.00	2,500.00
05/10/2002	752	Scanlan Wholesalers	202 · Accounts Payable	1,200.00	
		Scanlan Wholesalers	101 · Cash		1,200.00
				1,200.00	1,200.00
05/12/2002	534	Cody Slaton	122 · Accounts Receivable	3,150.00	
		Cody Slaton	401 · Sales		3,000.00
		Cody Slaton	231 · Sales Tax Payable		150.00
				3,150.00	3,150.00
05/12/2002			101 · Cash	2,100.00	
		Kori Reynolds	122 · Accounts Receivable		2,100.00
				2,100.00	2,100.00
05/13/2002	753	Simpson Enterprises	202 · Accounts Payable	1,500.00	
		Simpson Enterprises	101 · Cash		1,470.00
		Simpson Enterprises	501.2 · Purchases Discounts		30.00
				1,500.00	1,500.00
05/13/2002			401.1 · Sales Returns and Allowances	1,000.00	
			231 · Sales Tax Payable	50.00	
		Cody Slaton	122 · Accounts Receivable		1,050.00
				1,050.00	1,050.00
05/17/2002		Johnson Essentials	202 · Accounts Payable	500.00	
		Johnson Essentials	501.1 · Purchases Returns & Allowances		500.00
				500.00	500.00
05/22/2002			101 · Cash	1,555.00	
		Natalie Gabbert	122 · Accounts Receivable		1,555.00
				1,555.00	1,555.00

Page 1

13-D David's Specialty Shop
Journal
May 2002

Date	Num	Name	Account	Debit	Credit
05/27/2002	535	Natalie Gabbert	122 · Accounts Receivable	2,100.00	
		Natalie Gabbert	401 · Sales		2,000.00
		Natalie Gabbert	231 · Sales Tax Payable		100.00
				2,100.00	2,100.00
05/29/2002	754		542 · Wages Expense	1,100.00	
			101 · Cash		1,100.00
				1,100.00	1,100.00
TOTAL				**27,135.00**	**27,135.00**

13-D David's Specialty Shop
Trial Balance
As of May 31, 2002

	May 31, '02	
	Debit	Credit
101 · Cash	15,231.00	
122 · Accounts Receivable	7,045.00	
202 · Accounts Payable		4,050.00
231 · Sales Tax Payable		480.00
311 · David Kind, Capital		12,400.00
401 · Sales		10,600.00
401.1 · Sales Returns and Allowances	1,000.00	
501 · Purchases	3,500.00	
501.1 · Purchases Returns & Allowances		500.00
501.2 · Purchases Discounts		46.00
542 · Wages Expense	1,100.00	
545 · Telephone Expense	200.00	
TOTAL	**28,076.00**	**28,076.00**

13-D David's Specialty Shop
General Ledger
As of May 31, 2002

Date	Name	Account	Split	Amount	Balance
101 · Cash					10,050.00
05/02/2002	Kari Co.	101 · Cash	202 · Accounts Payable	-784.00	9,266.00
05/04/2002		101 · Cash	545 · Telephone Expense	-200.00	9,066.00
05/08/2002		101 · Cash	-SPLIT-	3,780.00	12,846.00
05/09/2002		101 · Cash	122 · Accounts Receivable	2,500.00	15,346.00
05/10/2002	Scanlan Whole...	101 · Cash	202 · Accounts Payable	-1,200.00	14,146.00
05/12/2002		101 · Cash	122 · Accounts Receivable	2,100.00	16,246.00
05/13/2002	Simpson Enterp...	101 · Cash	202 · Accounts Payable	-1,470.00	14,776.00
05/22/2002		101 · Cash	122 · Accounts Receivable	1,555.00	16,331.00
05/29/2002		101 · Cash	542 · Wages Expense	-1,100.00	15,231.00
Total 101 · Cash				5,181.00	15,231.00
122 · Accounts Receivable					6,900.00
05/01/2002	Molly Mac	122 · Accounts Rece...	-SPLIT-	2,100.00	9,000.00
05/09/2002	Cody Slaton	122 · Accounts Rece...	101 · Cash	-2,500.00	6,500.00
05/12/2002	Cody Slaton	122 · Accounts Rece...	-SPLIT-	3,150.00	9,650.00
05/12/2002	Kori Reynolds	122 · Accounts Rece...	101 · Cash	-2,100.00	7,550.00
05/13/2002	Cody Slaton	122 · Accounts Rece...	401.1 · Sales Returns an...	-1,050.00	6,500.00
05/22/2002	Natalie Gabbert	122 · Accounts Rece...	101 · Cash	-1,555.00	4,945.00
05/27/2002	Natalie Gabbert	122 · Accounts Rece...	-SPLIT-	2,100.00	7,045.00
Total 122 · Accounts Receivable				145.00	7,045.00
202 · Accounts Payable					-4,550.00
05/02/2002	Kari Co.	202 · Accounts Paya...	-SPLIT-	800.00	-3,750.00
05/03/2002	Scanlan Whole...	202 · Accounts Paya...	501 · Purchases	-2,000.00	-5,750.00
05/04/2002	Simpson Enterp...	202 · Accounts Paya...	501 · Purchases	-1,500.00	-7,250.00
05/10/2002	Scanlan Whole...	202 · Accounts Paya...	101 · Cash	1,200.00	-6,050.00
05/13/2002	Simpson Enterp...	202 · Accounts Paya...	-SPLIT-	1,500.00	-4,550.00
05/17/2002	Johnson Essen...	202 · Accounts Paya...	501.1 · Purchases Retur...	500.00	-4,050.00
Total 202 · Accounts Payable				500.00	-4,050.00
231 · Sales Tax Payable					0.00
05/01/2002	Molly Mac	231 · Sales Tax Pay...	122 · Accounts Receivable	-100.00	-100.00
05/08/2002		231 · Sales Tax Pay...	101 · Cash	-180.00	-280.00
05/12/2002	Cody Slaton	231 · Sales Tax Pay...	122 · Accounts Receivable	-150.00	-430.00
05/13/2002		231 · Sales Tax Pay...	401.1 · Sales Returns an...	50.00	-380.00
05/27/2002	Natalie Gabbert	231 · Sales Tax Pay...	122 · Accounts Receivable	-100.00	-480.00
Total 231 · Sales Tax Payable				-480.00	-480.00
311 · David Kind, Capital					-12,400.00
Total 311 · David Kind, Capital					-12,400.00
401 · Sales					0.00
05/01/2002	Molly Mac	401 · Sales	122 · Accounts Receivable	-2,000.00	-2,000.00
05/08/2002		401 · Sales	101 · Cash	-3,600.00	-5,600.00
05/12/2002	Cody Slaton	401 · Sales	122 · Accounts Receivable	-3,000.00	-8,600.00
05/27/2002	Natalie Gabbert	401 · Sales	122 · Accounts Receivable	-2,000.00	-10,600.00
Total 401 · Sales				-10,600.00	-10,600.00
401.1 · Sales Returns and Allowances					0.00
05/13/2002		401.1 · Sales Return...	-SPLIT-	1,000.00	1,000.00
Total 401.1 · Sales Returns and Allowances				1,000.00	1,000.00
501 · Purchases					0.00
05/03/2002		501 · Purchases	202 · Accounts Payable	2,000.00	2,000.00
05/04/2002		501 · Purchases	202 · Accounts Payable	1,500.00	3,500.00
Total 501 · Purchases				3,500.00	3,500.00
501.1 · Purchases Returns & Allowances					0.00
05/17/2002	Johnson Essen...	501.1 · Purchases R...	202 · Accounts Payable	-500.00	-500.00
Total 501.1 · Purchases Returns & Allowances				-500.00	-500.00

13-D David's Specialty Shop
General Ledger
As of May 31, 2002

Date	Name	Account	Split	Amount	Balance
501.2 · Purchases Discounts					0.00
05/02/2002	Kari Co.	501.2 · Purchases D...	202 · Accounts Payable	-16.00	-16.00
05/13/2002	Simpson Enterp...	501.2 · Purchases D...	202 · Accounts Payable	-30.00	-46.00
Total 501.2 · Purchases Discounts				-46.00	-46.00
542 · Wages Expense					0.00
05/29/2002		542 · Wages Expense	101 · Cash	1,100.00	1,100.00
Total 542 · Wages Expense				1,100.00	1,100.00
545 · Telephone Expense					0.00
05/04/2002		545 · Telephone Exp...	101 · Cash	200.00	200.00
Total 545 · Telephone Expense				200.00	200.00
TOTAL				**0.00**	**0.00**

13-D David's Specialty Shop
Customer Balance Summary
As of May 31, 2002

	May 31, '02
Cody Slaton	2,100.00
Kori Reynolds	200.00
Molly Mac	2,379.00
Natalie Gabbert	2,366.00
TOTAL	**7,045.00**

13-D David's Specialty Shop
Vendor Balance Summary
As of May 31, 2002

	May 31, '02
Johnson Essentials	1,850.00
Kari Co.	200.00
Scanlan Wholesalers	2,000.00
TOTAL	**4,050.00**

14-D Harpo, Inc.
Journal
March 2002

Type	Date	Num	Name	Account	Debit	Credit
Bill	03/02/2002	313	Tremont Rental	202 · Vouchers Payable		500.00
			Tremont Rental	521 · Rent Expense	500.00	
					500.00	500.00
Bill	03/03/2002	314	Gail's Gags	202 · Vouchers Payable		550.00
			Gail's Gags	501 · Purchases	550.00	
					550.00	550.00
Bill	03/04/2002	315	Silly Sam's	202 · Vouchers Payable		200.00
			Silly Sam's	501 · Purchases	200.00	
					200.00	200.00
Bill	03/16/2002	316	Giggles	202 · Vouchers Payable		700.00
			Giggles	501 · Purchases	700.00	
					700.00	700.00
Bill	03/21/2002	317	Creations	202 · Vouchers Payable		870.00
			Creations	501 · Purchases	870.00	
					870.00	870.00
Bill	03/25/2002	318	Hal's Supply	202 · Vouchers Payable		120.00
			Hal's Supply	141 · Supplies	120.00	
					120.00	120.00
Bill	03/31/2002	319	Payroll	202 · Vouchers Payable		1,250.00
			Payroll	511 · Wages Expense	1,250.00	
					1,250.00	1,250.00
TOTAL					**4,190.00**	**4,190.00**

14-D Harpo, Inc.
Journal
March 2002

Type	Date	Num	Name	Memo	Account	Debit	Credit
Check	03/02/2002	450	Tremont Rental	Voucher 313	101 · Cash		500.00
			Tremont Rental	Voucher 313	202 · Vouchers Payable	500.00	
						500.00	500.00
Check	03/10/2002	451	Jerry's Jokes	Voucher 310	101 · Cash		490.00
			Jerry's Jokes	Voucher 310	202 · Vouchers Payable	500.00	
			Jerry's Jokes	Voucher 310	501.2 · Purchases Discou...		10.00
						500.00	500.00
Check	03/14/2002	452	Resource Supplies	Voucher 311	101 · Cash		250.00
			Resource Supplies	Voucher 311	202 · Vouchers Payable	250.00	
						250.00	250.00
Check	03/18/2002	453	Gail's Gags	Voucher 314	101 · Cash		539.00
			Gail's Gags	Voucher 314	202 · Vouchers Payable	550.00	
			Gail's Gags	Voucher 314	501.2 · Purchases Discou...		11.00
						550.00	550.00
Check	03/19/2002	454	Donnelly's	Voucher 312	101 · Cash		750.00
			Donnelly's	Voucher 312	202 · Vouchers Payable	750.00	
						750.00	750.00
Check	03/31/2002	455	Silly Sam's	Voucher 315	101 · Cash		100.00
			Silly Sam's	Voucher 315	202 · Vouchers Payable	100.00	
						100.00	100.00
Check	03/31/2002	456	Payroll	Voucher 319	101 · Cash		1,250.00
			Payroll	Voucher 319	202 · Vouchers Payable	1,250.00	
						1,250.00	1,250.00
TOTAL						**3,900.00**	**3,900.00**

14-D Harpo, Inc.
Journal
March 12, 2002

Date	Name	Account	Debit	Credit
03/12/2002	Silly Sam's	202 · Vouchers Payable	100.00	
	Silly Sam's	501.1 · Purchases Returns & Allowance		100.00
			100.00	100.00
TOTAL			**100.00**	**100.00**

14-D Harpo, Inc.
Trial Balance
As of March 31, 2002

	Mar 31, '02	
	Debit	Credit
101 · Cash	2,121.00	
131 · Merchandise Inventory	8,425.00	
141 · Supplies	520.00	
202 · Vouchers Payable		1,690.00
311 · Retained Earnings		14,639.00
312 · Cash Dividends	1,500.00	
313 · Stock Dividends	3,000.00	
401 · Sales		10,786.00
501 · Purchases	6,570.00	
501.1 · Purchases Returns & Allowance		200.00
501.2 · Purchases Discounts		71.00
511 · Wages Expense	3,750.00	
521 · Rent Expense	1,500.00	
TOTAL	**27,386.00**	**27,386.00**

General Ledger
As of March 31, 2002

Type	Date	Name	Memo	Amount	Balance
101 · Cash					6,000.00
Check	03/02/2002	Tremont Rental	Voucher 313	-500.00	5,500.00
Check	03/10/2002	Jerry's Jokes	Voucher 310	-490.00	5,010.00
Check	03/14/2002	Resource Supplies	Voucher 311	-250.00	4,760.00
Check	03/18/2002	Gail's Gags	Voucher 314	-539.00	4,221.00
Check	03/19/2002	Donnelly's	Voucher 312	-750.00	3,471.00
Check	03/31/2002	Silly Sam's	Voucher 315	-100.00	3,371.00
Check	03/31/2002	Payroll	Voucher 319	-1,250.00	2,121.00
Total 101 · Cash				-3,879.00	2,121.00
131 · Merchandise Inventory					8,425.00
Total 131 · Merchandise Inventory					8,425.00
141 · Supplies					400.00
Bill	03/25/2002	Hal's Supply		120.00	520.00
Total 141 · Supplies				120.00	520.00
202 · Vouchers Payable					-1,500.00
Bill	03/02/2002	Tremont Rental		-500.00	-2,000.00
Check	03/02/2002	Tremont Rental	Voucher 313	500.00	-1,500.00
Bill	03/03/2002	Gail's Gags		-550.00	-2,050.00
Bill	03/04/2002	Silly Sam's		-200.00	-2,250.00
Check	03/10/2002	Jerry's Jokes	Voucher 310	500.00	-1,750.00
General Jour...	03/12/2002	Silly Sam's		100.00	-1,650.00
Check	03/14/2002	Resource Supplies	Voucher 311	250.00	-1,400.00
Bill	03/16/2002	Giggles		-700.00	-2,100.00
Check	03/18/2002	Gail's Gags	Voucher 314	550.00	-1,550.00
Check	03/19/2002	Donnelly's	Voucher 312	750.00	-800.00
Bill	03/21/2002	Creations		-870.00	-1,670.00
Bill	03/25/2002	Hal's Supply		-120.00	-1,790.00
Bill	03/31/2002	Payroll		-1,250.00	-3,040.00
Check	03/31/2002	Silly Sam's	Voucher 315	100.00	-2,940.00
Check	03/31/2002	Payroll	Voucher 319	1,250.00	-1,690.00
Total 202 · Vouchers Payable				-190.00	-1,690.00
311 · Retained Earnings					-14,639.00
Total 311 · Retained Earnings					-14,639.00
312 · Cash Dividends					1,500.00
Total 312 · Cash Dividends					1,500.00
313 · Stock Dividends					3,000.00
Total 313 · Stock Dividends					3,000.00
401 · Sales					-10,786.00
Total 401 · Sales					-10,786.00
501 · Purchases					4,250.00
Bill	03/03/2002	Gail's Gags		550.00	4,800.00
Bill	03/04/2002	Silly Sam's		200.00	5,000.00
Bill	03/16/2002	Giggles		700.00	5,700.00
Bill	03/21/2002	Creations		870.00	6,570.00
Total 501 · Purchases				2,320.00	6,570.00
501.1 · Purchases Returns & Allowance					-100.00
General Jour...	03/12/2002	Silly Sam's		-100.00	-200.00
Total 501.1 · Purchases Returns & Allowance				-100.00	-200.00
501.2 · Purchases Discounts					-50.00
Check	03/10/2002	Jerry's Jokes	Voucher 310	-10.00	-60.00
Check	03/18/2002	Gail's Gags	Voucher 314	-11.00	-71.00

14-D Harpo, Inc.
General Ledger
As of March 31, 2002

Type	Date	Name	Memo	Amount	Balance
Total 501.2 · Purchases Discounts				-21.00	-71.00
511 · Wages Expense					2,500.00
Bill	03/31/2002	Payroll		1,250.00	3,750.00
Total 511 · Wages Expense				1,250.00	3,750.00
521 · Rent Expense					1,000.00
Bill	03/02/2002	Tremont Rental		500.00	1,500.00
Total 521 · Rent Expense				500.00	1,500.00
TOTAL				**0.00**	**0.00**

14-D Harpo, Inc.
Vendor Balance Summary
As of March 31, 2002

	Mar 31, '02
Creations	870.00
Giggles	700.00
Hal's Supply	120.00
TOTAL	**1,690.00**

— 147 —

16-D McK's Home Electronics
Trial Balance
As of December 31, 2002

	Dec 31, '02	
	Debit	Credit
101 · Cash	10,000.00	
102 · Accounts Receivable	22,500.00	
131 · Merchandise Inventory	39,000.00	
141 · Supplies	2,700.00	
145 · Prepaid Insurance	3,600.00	
185 · Land	15,000.00	
190 · Building	135,000.00	
190.1 · Accum. Depreciation--Building		24,000.00
195 · Store Equipment	75,000.00	
195.1 · Accum. Depreciation--Store Eq.		22,500.00
201 · Notes Payable		7,500.00
202 · Accounts Payable		15,000.00
219 · Sales Tax Payable		2,250.00
241 · Unearned Repair Fees		18,000.00
285 · Mortgage Payable		45,000.00
311 · Tom McKinney, Capital		151,600.00
312 · Tom McKinney, Drawing	30,000.00	
401 · Sales		300,750.00
401.1 · Sales Returns and Allowances	1,800.00	
501 · Purchases	157,500.00	
501.1 · Purchases Returns & Allowances		1,200.00
501.2 · Purchases Discounts		1,500.00
502 · Freight-In	450.00	
511 · Wages Expense	63,000.00	
518 · Advertising Expense	3,750.00	
523 · Telephone Expense	5,250.00	
524 · Utilities Expense	18,000.00	
534 · Miscellaneous Expense	3,375.00	
537 · Interest Revenue		1,350.00
551 · Interest Expense	4,725.00	
TOTAL	**590,650.00**	**590,650.00**

16-D McK's Home Electronics
Journal
December 31, 2002

Date	Num	Account	Debit	Credit
12/31/2002	(a)	503 · Inventory Adjustment	39,000.00	
		131 · Merchandise Inventory		39,000.00
			39,000.00	39,000.00
12/31/2002	(b)	131 · Merchandise Inventory	45,000.00	
		503 · Inventory Adjustment		45,000.00
			45,000.00	45,000.00
12/31/2002	(c)	521 · Supplies Expense	2,100.00	
		141 · Supplies		2,100.00
			2,100.00	2,100.00
12/31/2002	(d)	527 · Insurance Expense	2,700.00	
		145 · Prepaid Insurance		2,700.00
			2,700.00	2,700.00
12/31/2002	(e)	529 · Depreciation Expense--Building	6,000.00	
		190.1 · Accum. Depreciation--Building		6,000.00
			6,000.00	6,000.00
12/31/2002	(f)	531 · Depreciation Expense--Store Eq.	4,500.00	
		195.1 · Accum. Depreciation--Store Eq.		4,500.00
			4,500.00	4,500.00
12/31/2002	(g)	511 · Wages Expense	675.00	
		214 · Wages Payable		675.00
			675.00	675.00
12/31/2002	(h)	241 · Unearned Repair Fees	15,000.00	
		535 · Repair Fees		15,000.00
			15,000.00	15,000.00
TOTAL			**114,975.00**	**114,975.00**

16-D McK's Home Electronics
Profit & Loss
December 2002

	Dec '02
Ordinary Income/Expense	
Income	
401 · Sales	300,750.00
401.1 · Sales Returns and Allowances	-1,800.00
Total Income	298,950.00
Cost of Goods Sold	
501 · Purchases	157,500.00
501.1 · Purchases Returns & Allowances	-1,200.00
501.2 · Purchases Discounts	-1,500.00
502 · Freight-In	450.00
503 · Inventory Adjustment	-6,000.00
Total COGS	149,250.00
Gross Profit	149,700.00
Expense	
511 · Wages Expense	63,675.00
518 · Advertising Expense	3,750.00
521 · Supplies Expense	2,100.00
523 · Telephone Expense	5,250.00
524 · Utilities Expense	18,000.00
527 · Insurance Expense	2,700.00
529 · Depreciation Expense--Building	6,000.00
531 · Depreciation Expense--Store Eq.	4,500.00
534 · Miscellaneous Expense	3,375.00
Total Expense	109,350.00
Net Ordinary Income	40,350.00
Other Income/Expense	
Other Income	
535 · Repair Fees	15,000.00
537 · Interest Revenue	1,350.00
Total Other Income	16,350.00
Other Expense	
551 · Interest Expense	4,725.00
Total Other Expense	4,725.00
Net Other Income	11,625.00
Net Income	**51,975.00**

16-D McK's Home Electronics
Balance Sheet
As of December 31, 2002

	Dec 31, '02
ASSETS	
Current Assets	
Checking/Savings	
101 · Cash	10,000.00
Total Checking/Savings	10,000.00
Other Current Assets	
102 · Accounts Receivable	22,500.00
131 · Merchandise Inventory	45,000.00
141 · Supplies	600.00
145 · Prepaid Insurance	900.00
Total Other Current Assets	69,000.00
Total Current Assets	79,000.00
Fixed Assets	
185 · Land	15,000.00
190 · Building	135,000.00
190.1 · Accum. Depreciation--Building	-30,000.00
195 · Store Equipment	75,000.00
195.1 · Accum. Depreciation--Store Eq.	-27,000.00
Total Fixed Assets	168,000.00
TOTAL ASSETS	**247,000.00**
LIABILITIES & EQUITY	
Liabilities	
Current Liabilities	
Other Current Liabilities	
201 · Notes Payable	7,500.00
202 · Accounts Payable	15,000.00
214 · Wages Payable	675.00
219 · Sales Tax Payable	2,250.00
241 · Unearned Repair Fees	3,000.00
Total Other Current Liabilities	28,425.00
Total Current Liabilities	28,425.00
Long Term Liabilities	
285 · Mortgage Payable	45,000.00
Total Long Term Liabilities	45,000.00
Total Liabilities	73,425.00
Equity	
311 · Tom McKinney, Capital	151,600.00
312 · Tom McKinney, Drawing	-30,000.00
Net Income	51,975.00
Total Equity	173,575.00
TOTAL LIABILITIES & EQUITY	**247,000.00**

16-D McK's Home Electronics
Trial Balance
As of January 1, 2003

	Jan 1, '03	
	Debit	Credit
101 · Cash	10,000.00	
102 · Accounts Receivable	22,500.00	
131 · Merchandise Inventory	45,000.00	
141 · Supplies	600.00	
145 · Prepaid Insurance	900.00	
185 · Land	15,000.00	
190 · Building	135,000.00	
190.1 · Accum. Depreciation--Building		30,000.00
195 · Store Equipment	75,000.00	
195.1 · Accum. Depreciation--Store Eq.		27,000.00
201 · Notes Payable		7,500.00
202 · Accounts Payable		15,000.00
214 · Wages Payable		675.00
219 · Sales Tax Payable		2,250.00
241 · Unearned Repair Fees		3,000.00
285 · Mortgage Payable		45,000.00
311 · Tom McKinney, Capital		173,575.00
TOTAL	**304,000.00**	**304,000.00**

16-D McK's Home Electronics
Journal
January 1, 2003

Date	Num	Account	Debit	Credit
01/01/2003	Rev.Ent.	214 · Wages Payable	675.00	
		535 · Repair Fees		675.00
			675.00	675.00
TOTAL			**675.00**	**675.00**